Alessandro Gualtieri – Giovanni Dalle Fusine

# An Italian Forever
*Tales from the manslaughters of the Isonzo River,*
*Caporetto and the Great War*

LediPublishing

© 2009 Ledizioni LediPublishing
Via Alamanni 11 – 20141 Milano – Italy
http://www.ledipublishing.com
info@ledipublishing.com

Translated from: "Dal Piave alla Prigionia. L'odissea del soldato Settimio Damiani Gennaio 1914 - Agosto 1919"
Nordpress Edizioni
Translated by: Alessandro Gualtieri

First Edition: February 2009

ISBN 978-88-95994-04-8

All rights reserved. No part of this publication may be reproduced, stored in a retrieval system, transmitted or utilized in any form or by any means, electronic, mechanical, photocopying or otherwise, without permission in writing from the publisher.

*«A lie can travel halfway round the world while the truth is putting on its shoes».*
*Mark Twain*

# Index

| | |
|---|---|
| Foreword | 9 |
| Introduction | 13 |
| An ordinary hero in the hell of the great war | 18 |
| A brief history of the first world war | 24 |
| Summer 1916 – In the warzone | 28 |
| Convalescence with the siena Brigade in Valsugana | 55 |
| Campaign of 1917 | 68 |
| The tenth battle of the Isonzo | 72 |
| The eleventh battle of the Isonzo | 94 |
| The Caporetto rout | 104 |
| Imprisonment | 112 |
| Appendix 1 - The medals awarded to Settimio Damiani | 125 |
| Glossary | 131 |
| Bibliography | 134 |
| Acknowledgments | 137 |

# Foreword

We were all too busy with our personal lives and struggles to notice. The importance of our father's diary evolved over many years. Looking back, did we know it even existed? If we knew, we didn't place any importance on it. As the years went by, four events changed our perspective.

First, an article in the factory newsletter, where he worked, referred to a diary. Our father worked in the Maintenance Department of a glass container factory in Chicago Heights, Illinois, 30 miles south of Chicago. I (Chet) worked there, too, in the Storeroom. His Foreman was Angelo Primavera who wrote a monthly newsletter for the factory employees. I recall Angelo shouting out every morning at the start of work «Andiamo, Andiamo» («let's go, let's go») as the men were milling about.

Angelo interviewed different employees to get stories for his monthly newsletter. Around 1957 an article appeared in the newsletter and mentioned the diary our father had written in Italy as an Italian soldier in The Great War of 1914-1919. An off hand remark in the article «this should make interesting reading» piqued my interest years later. Our father never talked to his family about the diary. If he did, it went in one ear and out the other. We do not recall any conversation about his war experience. When questioning our older brother, Ted, (Eleuterio) all he remembered was Dad saying the best meal he had was potato skins one time during incarceration in the concentration camp. That newsletter turned out to be a turning point in a chain of events.

The second event was when we learned Ernest Hemmingway's bestseller, A Farewell to Arms, talked about the same battle our father, Settimio, fought in.

A third point was when our brother, Guy (Gaetano) found the diary in a basement which had flooded. That was approximately 25 years after our father's death. I can just picture Guy walking in puddles of water on a rainy night wearing his Greek/Italian fisherman's cap, tilted to one side, and then walking down the basement steps. It was a wonder he even found the diary because our father had died several years before, and our stepmother, Rosa, had a penchant for tossing things out. She was a minimalist and didn't like odd things lying around. Little by little the diary started to gain momentum.

My son Tim liked to spend time with our father. As a child, Tim would often go over to our father's home, about 5 houses down the street, and they would have chats. Perhaps this bond between Tim and his grandfather was the catalyst that made it all happen. Years later when the adult Tim learned about the diary, he asked about it. I had a copy, intending to search for a college professor who specialized in Italian history so it could be translated in English. It was written in Italian and not an easy read due to dialect, geographical references, etc. I became discouraged when a university professor, I had contacted for translation help, did not return my calls. Tim, however, was more tenacious. Through the internet, he found a history scholar who had studied and done research on The Great War, wrote a book about it, and created a marvelous website (http://www.lagrandeguerra.net). We struck gold in this find! Alessandro Gualtieri, who lives half way across the globe in Milan was shown the battlefields of the Great War by his grandmother when he was just a child. From this, a life long passion to learn all he could about Italian war history has guided his life as a scholar. All of his research and writing is about the Great War. For Alessandro, our father's diary is a golden key to history's secrets.

Few Italians could read and write in those days. Our father wrote about this war in great detail just as it was happening.

We often have wondered where our father got the idea to journal. Was it from another soldier? Was it his way to keep his sanity?

After the traumatic experiences of this mortal combat, our father never took food or kindness for granted. He savored both. He was very appreciative of nurses and staff who treated his wounds in a Red Cross Hospital in northern Italy. To the day he died, he always wanted to give a little something extra for the nurses and aids who cared for him in the nursing home.

His extremely strong work ethic was a solid part of his character. He was the one sent into the blazing hot furnaces of the glass factory to repair the bricks in the roof of the furnaces, dressed in his spaceman-like asbestos suit. A Supervisor was once asked why he chose certain men to do important jobs. He said in his street wise vernacular, «you always ride the horse that runs».

This dedication, tenacity, and determination may have been what kept him alive during those horrible war years. Thousands of his comrades didn't make it. Lives were extinguished before his eyes. He did not share any of it with his family. It was too hard to relive. Almost 100 years later, it is equally hard to read. If I hated war before, I abhor it after reading these plain words of our hero, Settimio Damiani.

It turned otherwise decent men into monsters and led thousands upon thousands of young men to slaughter.

Through this wonderful diary, we have been given back our father, a quiet man who speaks to us now. He has become our hero, a brave young man who faced imminent death constantly and gave his all to his comrades. This is the spirit of Settimio Damiani which he left with us.

Chester (Cesare) Damiani

Lee (Nicolena Damiani) Malizia

# Introduction

Quite often the public gets to know a famous person in history through the personal diaries and memories he or she left us, after leaving this world. In spite of biographies, these personal accounts, originally written for personal reference and use only, are the best way to discover the real personality of the author. Many characters of the Great War make no exception and, in the course of almost one century, a large number of diaries and similar publications have reached a bigger and bigger audience throughout the world. Nonetheless, most of these books have originated from the memories of war veterans and occasional research, while the personal diary of Settimio Damiani has a sensibly greater and most exclusive value for us. Apart from inevitable mistakes in his yet still powerful grammar, our protagonist wrote only first person eye-witness accounts in real time, rather than compiling a mere book of some long-gone memories years after the end of the war. His work is not an exercise of memory but a real, striking report «live» from the battlefield; he is holding a still-smoking rifle in the left hand and his trustworthy pen in the other. Settimio's thoughts and unabridged emotions are therefore preserved in their full, spontaneous integrity and immediately recorded on the battered pages of his notebook.

Comparing the propaganda of that era and the official communiqués with Settimio's records and account, a comprehensive and more «human» picture of the war emerges from the fog of time. Settimio's point of view is inevitably limited by the narrow slits of a trench parapet and hampered by lice, vermin, and foul smelling shelters, but still it proves much more vivid, realistic, and priceless as a unique memory of such a ghastly past.

Just as it happens on the silver screen, bombs and nerve-shattering artillery blasts, cries of wounded comrades, and the terrible «sounds» of battle are intertwined in Settimio's accounts as a tragic soundtrack which dramatically helps bring the whole story alive, and tragically kicking in our hearts as well as in our imagination.

The writing skills of our protagonist are also quite unusual, especially considering that back in 1914–1918, Italy reported about 70% of analphabetism, and Le Marche region where Settimio was from, ranked amongst the very first with this percentage.
The need to record all his feelings, emotions, and memories in a personal diary appears tenfold for Settimio Damiani. He surely always kept his trustworthy notebook as a good–luck charm and as a unique bond to the real world, miles away from the terrifying battle zones. It surely served him also as a way to «decompress» after a particularly moving or nerve–shattering event and the perfect remedy to fight desperation, solitude, and despair. The overall picture of what has been so painstakingly and comprehensively recorded in the diary is a most touching one: Settimio Damiani has left us so much more than war memories – his legacy, of blood, honor, loyalty, sacrifice, hardship, and pain, is there, permanently embedded in the very texture of one century–old yellowing pages.

According to the official military records, we now know for sure that the very first page of the diary is not the actual first day in combat for Settimio Damiani. Back in 1916 the «Roma» infantry Brigade has already been stationing its men on the Italian front lines for at least one full year. Soldiers are then ready to repel any possible Austro–Hungaric invasion.

It would be even too easy to assume that the actual first pages of the diary have been lost, but on second thought, Settimio may have decided to emulate a writer friend, met in the trenches of Mount Majo in the first months of active service. Settimio Damiani's point of view is surely hampered by his rural, humble origins – he does not fight the politicians' war but rather his very own struggle for surviving every single challenge of life. He simply does everything humanly possible to save himself from strafing bullets, annihilating shells, and the craziness of mankind at war.
At this point, his barely intelligible Italian is more than enough to condemn the mindless ego of military commanders and the lethal greediness of politicians who squeezed out from their puppet–like armies the very last ounce of sweat and blood and then merely conquered only a square mile of barren and useless terrain. But in every single attack and even in each most trivial action, Settimio found a reason for challenging death to get one mile nearer home, his family, and loved ones.

For unknown reasons, after recording the months of imprisonment, the diary ends abruptly. It's important to remember how difficult it must

il fuoco di artiglieria è incessante. i camminamenti che sono profondi due metri, è un passaggio insopportabile, ogni tanto bisogna sostare per far passare barelle con feriti; qualche piede scivola sopra ai corpi umani, caduti mortalmente dentro ai camminamenti, sopra non si può salire e scoperti. è un vero terrore, portano dei morti insopportabile. Non credevo che il carso era una lotta tanto accanito la nostra offensiva prose...

The original diary of Settimio Damiani, incredibly well-preserved after almost one century. It was written during the war, with daily entries full of striking accounts about the author's terrible ordeal. The Damiani family managed to save it from a basement which had flooded. Actually it was a wonder they even found the diary because some family members had a penchant for tossing old things out. The diary is in the hands of the living relatives of Settimio Damiani, in Chicago Heights, IL, USA.

anche alla prima linea con granate di grosso calibro, specialmente le bombarde fanno certi schianti vecchi e cosa di spavento. i camminamenti son tutti sconvolti, sotterrati anche cadaveri per i camminamenti. e un vero terrore e cosa di morire chi non anno mai veduto. Il 27 agosto due plotone cianno portato alla dolina modena agregato al genio per trasporto materiale. tutte le sere passando per la strada di...

have been for a barely-dressed and poorly-fed Settimio to keep his diary in the pure hell of concentration camps during the heart of winter 1917–1918. Prisoners were not allowed any personal possession, nor any particular item for personal use or comfort; therefore Settimio had to hide his pen and notebook very carefully, thereby taking very dangerous chances and risking hard punishment on a daily basis.

No word is recorded about the eventual liberation from the prison camp – such event simply took place without any particular mention – only the official military records help us find Settimio later re-installed in the 84th Infantry Regiment on January 8th, 1919. At that time, he was ready to face other challenges and move on with his life. He gave so much to his country, but the diary was lost in oblivion for some 90 years.

After months of thorough research, in national and private archives, as well as in old and dusty bookstores, and even flea-markets, (not to mention the outstanding support offered by some members of the Damiani family) the authors of this book were able to collate together the whole historical scenario which now serves as the ideal background for the original diary left by Settimio Damiani. But the real, undisputed credits are all for the humble and brave infantryman-writer from Acquaviva Picena – it's Settimio Damiani who decided to leave us such a priceless and unique account of that war, that era and most of all, of that particular moment in his life.

# An ordinary hero in the hell of the great war

Settimio Damiani was born on October 2$^{nd}$, 1890, in the little town of Acquaviva Picena, in Le Marche Region, Italy. Settimio («the Seventh») was born after his six brothers: Achille, Cesare, Gaetano, Nicola, Serafino and Filippo. Settimio's parents were Eleuterio Damiani and Francesca Pignati. Until the age of 18, Settimio worked in the fields around his hometown and had a chance to try his luck in the U.S., where he moved, along with his brother, Achille, in 1909. Achille became a labor broker and head of the Hod Carriers Union Local 5. The brothers worked in construction and assisted the brick layers. Eventually they ended up working in factories.

Soon, Settimio and Achille were joined by Cesare, Gaetano, and their cousin Domenico Sabatini. Business was good and Settimio and Gaetano seriously considered becoming U.S. citizens, officially filing their request with the American authorities on November 13$^{th}$, 1913. At the time, this was one of the first steps one had to take in order to apply for US citizenship. Soon after that (possibly within a month) Settimio Damiani returned to Italy to carry out his military service obligation. Gaetano, on the other hand, stayed behind and later ended up being drafted into the US Army in 1916 and was deployed to France with the US Army's 7th division. While in France, he was poisoned during a mustard-gas attack and later died from complications related to that injury on June 15$^{th}$, 1931. Gaetano is buried in the same cemetery where his brother Settimio as well as other members of the Damiani family rest. His grave, however, is in a section reserved for war veterans.

Cesare returned to Italy to fulfill his military service obligation and recent researches point to a premature death in combat, during the Italian–Libyan war; a special award medal was granted to the Damianis in 1922.

But let's go back to the main character of our incredible story. Settimio

Settimio Damiani in 1914, when he was enrolled in the Italian Army. When he spontaneously returned to Italy to carry out his military service obligation he was punished with some months of imprisonment for being late, and then sent immediately to the front lines.

Damiani was trained as a soldier in Italy and then, at the outbreak of WWI between his home country and Austria–Hungary, he was sent up in the very front lines, north of the Asiago Plateau. Settimio started keeping a personal diary in which he recorded, up to the very end of the war (spent in Austrian and German P.O.W. camps), all his terrible experiences as a front line infantryman. The diary is incredibly detailed and very well written, especially when considering that back at the beginning of the last century, very few people in Italy (about 5–7 %) could actually read and express their emotions and feelings in writings. As a real patriot and a humble, «ordinary hero», Settimio took part in intense and heavy fighting, first on the Trentino salient, then on the Isonzo river where the Italian generals pushed the most for invading enemy territories, while obtaining minimum territorial gains drenched in terrible manslaughter and absurd bloodbath. After all, the so called Great War was intended as the «War of Material» where battles were allegedly won by simply sending thousands of young soldiers to the slaughter. The balance of power has never been so brutally set.

Comprehensive and detailed research points to Settimio obtaining the rank of corporal at some time during the war, although there is no official record about this well–deserved promotion. He did his job quite thoroughly and in a most dedicated way, often risking his life for his comrades before thinking about himself.

Eventually, Settimio had to fight his last battle, tasked with the impossible mission of repelling the Austro–German push during the infamous rout of the Italian Army at Caporetto, in November 1917, as vividly depicted in Hemingway's Farewell To Arms. Settimio did his very best but was eventually surrounded and taken prisoner by the enemy. From then on, he had to endure a terrible hardship while spending more than a year in at least three concentration camps. He suffered from famine, disease, and, most of all, the cold, since he was barely able to cover himself with simple sheets of paper! Still, he never gave up writing his diary, even when he was forced to barter his trustworthy pen for a couple of crackers!

Eventually, in late 1918, Settimio was transferred to a fortress–prison in Salzburg, Austria, where he proved his craftsmanship and was therefore allowed to work along with civilians, thus slightly improving his conditions as a prisoner of war.

In 1919 Settimio was released and came back to Italy. He married Federica Silenzi from San Benedetto del Tronto and had his first child, Eleuterio. Shortly after Eleuterio's birth, Settimio returned to Chicago

Heights to rejoin Achille and look for work, leaving his wife and newborn son behind. He sent for them 5 years later, and they joined him in Chicago Heights in the summer of 1926. They ended up having 3 more children here in the United States: Cesare (Chet), Gaetano (Guy) and Nicolena (Lena).

In a short article published in his American factory's internal newspaper, Settimio Damiani was depicted as a good man, trustworthy, highly skilled, and reliable. We can say that Settimio was a no–nonsense hard worker who faced every single challenge in his life, no matter how hard and demanding with undisputed and indomitable willpower and sheer dedication.

His first son, Eleuterio, joined the U.S. Air Force and was on a troop ship on December 7th, 1941, on the way to Pearl Harbor and had to turn around because of the bombing. His next son, Cesare, fought for 10 months in the Korean War. Before becoming a university teacher in Chicago, Gaetano served in the Army in Germany.

Before passing away, on January 1st, 1979, Settimio Damiani had a chance to get to know his grandson Tim, Cesare's son, to whom he told the tale of his terrible war experiences while the young kid listened in total awe. Tim later discovered the original diary written by his granddad but, in spite of his Italian roots, he could never discern nor understand the approximate 80 pages of thick and nervous calligraphy.

The Diary itself has its own story. Gaetano, the university teacher was a linguist but even he couldn't decipher it. His brother Chet told him not to lose it because it was a historical document and also that it covered the same battle Ernest Hemingway depicted in Farewell to Arms. Chet even contacted a professor at Loyola University in Chicago who is versed in Italian history but, when he never returned his call, he became discouraged. Eventually, Tim Damiani, Nicolena's nephew, came into possession of the diary. Again, in spite of more painstaking efforts, no one could interpret it nor seemed interested enough. Everybody tried, but Tim is the one who did not give up and today, because of his tenacity, the whole Damiani family is grateful to him and to the Italian historian who eventually decrypted the diary.

Tim contacted an Italian website entirely dedicated to the First World War and run by Italian historian and writer Alessandro Gualtieri (http://www.lagrandeguerra.net), seeking help for the translation of the diary. Mr. Gualtieri welcomed such a unique chance to read such an in–depth, first person account and soon decided to start thorough research to eventually make a real book out of Settimio's incredible experiences.

Mr. Alessandro Gualtieri, co-authoring the book with another WWI Italian historian and journalist, Mr. Giovanni Dalle Fusine, is currently also trying to locate and present the Damiani family with the two medals of honor granted to Settimio in 1920 and also the third one, given to the Damianis in recognition of his brother Cesare's death in combat. Those awards were in fact never collected by Settimio who returned to the U.S. before the Italian Government officialized them in 1922.

# MEET SETTIMIO DAMIANI
## by Angelo Primavera

Settimio was born on October 2, 1891 in Aqua Viva, on the Adriatic side of Italy. He had a very quiet childhood. In those days very few children had an opportunity to go to school, but Sett was more fortunate than others. He was able to get a grade school education. In Italy, as was the case in most European countries, if you were able to read or write you were considered an educated man.

Sett came to this country in 1908 when only 17 years old, and in 1913 he went back to Italy to serve his hitch in the army. In the meantime World War I broke out and he had to spend seven years in the service. He fought with the infantry and was wounded several times and received the equivalent of our Purple Heart decoration in Italy. He was captured on the Austrian border when Germany entered the war and was held prisoner for 13 months in Germany. While he was a prisoner of war he wrote a diary which should make some interesting reading.

Sett married after the war in San Benedetto, Italy. San Benedetto is a famous Italian summer resort on the Adriatic Sea and Sett's hometown is just a few miles away. He came back to U.S.A. alone in 1921. A son, Teddy, was born in Italy while Sett was here and five years later he sent for his wife and son.

Sett has four brothers, all in Italy. Sett also has three boys, one girl, and two grandchildren. Teddy, who was born in Italy and now lives in Chicago, was in the Air Force, and was half way across the Pacific when Pearl Harbor was attacked. Chester, who works in our Storeroom, was in Korea during that campaign and spent about ten months there. Guy went to Northern Illinois Teachers college and to the University of Chicago for a Master's degree. At this writing he is awaiting an assignment to teach Spanish in an Illinois High School. Sett's married daughter Lena, has two children, Rita Lynn and a new daughter Julie, born June 24, missing her mother's birthday by one day.

Sett's first wife, Rita, died in 1946. He remarried in 1952; his wife, Rosa is from San Pedro, Italy although Sett met Rosa here.

As a hobby Sett does a little gardening and loves to watch T.V. For his sports activity he likes to play "Bocce" and enjoys playing "Morra." He is hardly ever without an Italian stogie in his mouth, though it is seldom lit.

He worked as a mason's helper on construction before coming to Kimble Glass. He came here to work on a furnace rebuild in 1941 and stayed with us.

Sett tells about the time he went back to Italy to serve his hitch in the army. In those days all Italian subjects were duty bound to return to their native land when their age group was eligible to serve in the armed forces. No matter when you went back you would be arrested for deserting. Sett went back three years after his group was called and he was court martialed, but in view of the circumstances was only put on probation for six months.

SETTIMIO DAMIANI

This article was published in the monthly newsletter of the factory where Settimio Damiani worked after the Great War. It was written by his foreman, Angelo Primavera.

# A brief history of the first world war

World War I, also known as the First World War, the Great War, and the War To End All Wars, was a global military conflict which took place primarily in Europe from 1914 to 1918. Over 40 million casualties resulted including approximately 20 million military and civilian deaths.

The immediate cause of the war was June 28$^{th}$, 1914, assassination of Archduke Franz Ferdinand, heir to the Austro–Hungarian throne, by Gavrilo Princip, a Bosnian Serb citizen of Austria–Hungary. The retaliation by Austria–Hungary against Serbia activated a series of alliances that set off a chain reaction of war declarations. Within a month, much of Europe was in a state of open warfare. The war was propagated by two major alliances. The Entente Powers initially consisted of France, the United Kingdom, Russia and their associated empires and dependencies. Numerous other states joined these allies, most notably Italy in May, 1915, and the United States in April, 1917. The Central Powers, so named because of their central location on the European continent, initially consisted of Germany and Austria–Hungary and their associated empires – including Italy, which signed the so–called Triple Alliance in 1882.

The Ottoman Empire joined the Central Powers in October, 1914, followed a year later by Bulgaria. By the conclusion of the war, only The Netherlands, Switzerland, Spain, and the Scandinavian nations remained officially neutral among the European countries though many of them provided financial and material support to one side or the other.

Italy, in particular, refused to enter the war to help Germany and Austria–Hungary, in August 1914, receding from the Triple Alliance with a simple, undisputable legal claim: it would have deployed its troops only in the case of an aggression against one of the other allies, but not in the case of the latter attacking and invading other countries. As we have seen, Italy remained neutral until May, 1915, when the Entente Powers offered Italy an unbeatable and tempting series of territorial gain, rewards for entering the conflict against the Central Powers.

The fighting of the war mostly took place along several fronts that broadly encircled the European continent. The Western Front was marked by a system of trenches, breastworks, and fortifications separated by an area known as no-man's-land.

These fortifications stretched 475 miles – more than 600 kilometers – from the Netherlands to Switzerland and precipitated a style of fighting known as trench warfare. On the Eastern Front, the vast eastern plains and limited rail network prevented a trench warfare stalemate, though the scale of the conflict was just as large as on the Western Front. The Middle Eastern Front and the Italian Front also saw heavy fighting, while hostilities also occurred at sea and, for the first time, in the air. The war was ended by several treaties, most notably the Treaty of Versailles, signed on June 28th, 1919, though the Allied powers had an armistice with Germany in place since November 11th, 1918.

One of the most striking results of the war was a large redrawing of the map of Europe. All of the Central Powers lost territory, and many new nations were created.

The resulting outcome of the war caused many changes.

The German Empire lost its colonial possessions and was saddled with accepting blame for the war as well as paying punitive reparations for it.

The Austro–Hungarian and Ottoman empires were completely dissolved.

Austria–Hungary was carved up into several successor states including Austria, Hungary, Czechoslovakia, and Yugoslavia.

The Ottoman Empire disintegrated, and much of its non–Anatolian territory was awarded as protectorates of various Allied powers, while the remaining Turkish core was reorganized as the Republic of Turkey.

The Russian Empire, which had withdrawn from the war in 1917, lost much of its western frontier as the newly independent nations of Estonia, Finland, Latvia, Lithuania, and Poland were carved from it.

After the war, the League of Nations was created as an international organization designed to avoid future wars by giving nations a means of solving their differences diplomatically.

World War I marked the end of the world order which had existed after the Napoleonic Wars and was an important factor in the outbreak of World War II.

## Italy and the Great War

Italy was totally unprepared for this massive venture. The Army was nowhere near being on the appropriate footing and money for armaments was scarce. Nevertheless, the Italian armies marched into Austrian territory in the northeast with some success against armed forces who had their hands full elsewhere.

The poorly–armed and badly–led peasant conscripts fought bravely on the Isonzo, in the Adige valley, and around Asiago. However, a prolonged stalemate quickly developed which was not broken until the end of 1917. Then the Austrians and Germans, freed from the burden of the Russian front, attacked and inflicted a humiliating defeat on the Italians at the Battle of Caporetto.

The Austro–German armies moved south to threaten the peninsula; Italy seemed to be in grave peril, and British and French troops were dispatched to the rescue.

The Italians, however, responded to the challenge with great fortitude and spirit. Before the arrival of the Allied forces, the greatly outnumbered Italian Army halted the Austro–German advance on the River Piave – a military feat which has gone down in nationalist folklore and which was celebrated in the patriotic song «Il Piave mormorò ... non passa lo straniero» («The Piave whispered ... the foreigner shall not pass...»). By the autumn of 1918, the Italian and Allied forces were driving the Austrians back towards the north. A notable victory was achieved at the Battle of Vittorio Veneto, and on November 4$^{th}$, 1918, an armistice was concluded with Austria and the war was over. Italy was on the winning side, but victory had been costly. The effort of mobilizing more than five million men over 3$^{1/2}$, years had involved great personal and financial sacrifice. There had been nearly 700,000 casualties. The longer–term cost for democracy in Italy however, was to be even greater. In the end, the gains from the war certainly did not justify the enormous cost since the Paris peace conference proved to be a massive comedown for the Italians. They had been foolish to place too much trust in a secret treaty drawn up in the middle of a war, because the US President Woodrow Wilson refused to recognize its validity, and the other Allies failed to support the demands of the indecisive and diplomatically naïve Italian representatives, Vittorio Emanuele Orlando and Sidney Sonnino.

In the Treaty of Versailles of January, 1920, Italy emerged with the promised important gains in the northeast section of the country up to the Brenner Pass and with some fairly useless territory in North Africa, but with none of the other territories promised in London. Nationalistic opinion in the country was infuriated by the settlement – Italy had won the war but had lost the peace. It was another nail in the coffin of the Liberal state.

# Summer 1916 – In the warzone

The «Punitive Expedition» (Strafeexpedition) was almost over and the Italians have been fighting on three different fronts, including the Lagarina and Cismon valleys, for slightly more than a year, ever since May 24$^{th}$, 1915. In particular, the enemy «Punitive Expedition» has been originally designed and fought to eventually break any Italian resistance and reach the Venetian plains from the southernmost ridge of the Asiago plateau. Here, the Austro–Hungaric imperial troops would have found plenty of well–stocked military depots and vital war materials previously allocated nearby the old borderline which the Italians crossed at the beginning of the war.

Right before the attack, the 79$^{th}$ infantry Regiment in which Settimio Damiani was serving, was part of the «Roma Brigade», along its twin–Regiment, the 80$^{th}$. The whole Brigade was deployed on the line from Vallarsa through the right end of the Terragnolo valley, along with the Alpine troops battalions «Val Leogra» and «Mount Berico» and the XII$^{nd}$ territorial infantry Brigade. All these units were commanded by the Italian 1$^{st}$ Army which in those days was some 230,000 men strong.

When the diary begins, Damiani has already been in the front line for one month, according also to his military records which recite: «Enrolled in the 79$^{th}$ infantry Regiment on May 24$^{th}$, 1916». On the night of May 23$^{rd}$, the «Roma» Brigade was transferred East of Pian delle Fugazze to replenish its many losses suffered during the previous battles. Because of a temporary lack of new recruits, it was possible to bring only one of its two Regiments up to full fighting force.

The front line was recently well consolidated on both sides. In the first hours of June 25$^{th}$ most of the attackers were still hidden away in the «winter line» shelters («Winterstellung»): a series of bunkers, caves and heavily defended entrenchments which the Italians would never capture

Settimio Damiani portrayed back in Chicago Heights, Illinois, after the Great War. His extremely strong professional ethic was a solid part of his character. Both during the war and after it he was often tasked with most difficult and demanding chores. A Supervisor was once asked why he chose certain men to do important jobs. He said in his street wise vernacular, «you always ride the horse that runs».

A moment of rest for Italian infantrymen in the trenches of the Carso Plateau. The mail has been recently distributed and the luckiest soldiers received a letter from home. Some of them produced personal diaries, but Settimio Damiani wrote only first person eye–witness accounts in real time, rather than compiling a mere book of some long–gone memories years after the end of the war.

until the very end of the Great War. On June 29th, both the 79th and the 80th regiments were moved to positions adjacent to the Leno di Vallarsa River, where they were employed in battle from June 9th through June 11th and thus re-capturing the rocky ridge of Parmesan. Ten days later, the entire Brigade became part of the 27th division and transferred to the Sogli di Campiglia–Colle di Xomo sector.

The «Punitive Expedition» developed by the Austrian Commander in Chief, Franz Conrad von Hötzendorf, caused the loss of more than 73,000 infantrymen and 23,000 officers in the Italian Army. These figures roughly double the casualties sustained by the enemy. The war did not end nor ceased to ask for more manslaughter; the front line Astico–Posina kept on being heavily pounded by artillery shells and bathed for more months to come in the blood of thousands of fighting men. Settimio Damiani actively witnessed and took part in the desperate defense of the line which ran from Mount Majo through the Sellette Mountains, reaching the peaks at 4,560 feet and 4,675 feet In particular, the Italian heavily armored trenches at 4,829 feet proved a most annoying and dangerous salient in the enemy line which the Austro–Hungarians could not overtake. From this height, the front line was following the Val Grande to the hamlet of Griso, thus climbing again to the peaks of the Pasubio Mountain Range.

The Austrians were entrenched on the north side of the Posina valley, strategically sheltered by Mount Cimone, Mount Seluggio, and Mount Tormeno. The main Italian line of resistance was set in the southernmost part of this area, across Mount Alba, Colletto di Posina, and Mount Spin, reaching Mount Novegno, Priaforà and Caviojo and thus guarding and blocking the access to the Arsiero valley.

The «Roma» Brigade was commanded by general Giuseppe Moccagatta until June 15th, 1916, when Vincenzo Rossi took his place. Settimio Damiani's 79th Regiment in particular, was lead by colonel Agostino Versace. During this particular spell of time, recorded in Settimio's diary on July 10th, the famous Italian patriots, Cesare Battisti and Fabio Filzi were captured and then hung by the Austrians. Although this tragic event took place on the nearby Mount Corno di Vallarsa, Settimio went totally unaware of it. Instead, the diary reports the rumble of a massive explosion in the distance, which Settimio heard on September 23rd, while hospitalized, when 32,000 pounds of TNT went off in the galleries of Mount Cimone; the Austrians dislodged the poor men of the «Sele» Brigade from upper positions and crests of the mountain, thus «remodeling it forever».

The «soldiers' laundry». Along the Posina Valley, near Fusine, the troopers in the picture are setting up «barber» and «laundry» services. The clothes hanging on a improvised line and the relaxed soldiers having a chat speak of the horrors of war as if they were a long-forgotten memory.

Infantryman Settimio Damiani during the Great War. His cap bears the insignia of the 84th Infantry Regiment of the «Venezia» Brigade.

Winter 1916, camouflaged Italian military huts in the Posina Valley. During the war many different forms of camouflage were created to conceal barracks and military installation. In this picture, the buildings are shrouded in by bamboo curtains and screens of thick cloth.

So, now we are on Mount Majo where a barren and quite hostile environment is beaten by blinding sunlight twelve months a year and scarce pine forests offer very poor protection. In the newspaper Giornale d'Italia dated May 4<sup>th</sup>, 1917, the journalist Achille Benedetti described this very mountain as: «... *an octopus–like, frozen entanglement of high peaks. Here, the Alpine troops are forced to hazardously climb every single step of the way, towards enemy lines, dangerously hampered by backpacks full of grenades and with their rifles hastily secured on their backs. They cannot afford to lose even one finger grip on the barren and slippery rocky sides of the mountain. It's a very nasty customer!*»

What nowadays are attractive tourist resorts a few miles away from the industrial city of Schio, there used to be the main depots and concentration area for Italian troops stationed in this sector. The many buildings somehow had survived the previous Austro–Hungarian offensive (the «Punitive Expedition») and had been converted to stores and barracks, while every single access route was carefully camouflaged. From the nearby enemy lines on the Mount Cimone very little activity could be observed. Through the hazardous and incredibly narrow paths originating from the hamlets of Cogollo del Cengio, Arsiero, Laghi, Posina, and Fusine, the Italian Generalissimo, Luigi Cadorna, managed to move incredible quantities of war material to first stop and then repel the enemy invasion. On those very roads, Settimio Damiani traveled with his backpack, his wooden canteen and his trustworthy '91 rifle.

Italian official war bulletins of that time recite: «*#403, July 1<sup>st</sup>,1916 – The Italian advance proceeded along the Posina Valley, in spite of the enemy artillery deluge from the upper positions of the Borcola Pass, Mount Maggio and Mount Toraro. On the left side of our lines, the troops climbed to the top of Mount Majo and from here they kept on pushing the enemy northward*».

«*#404, July 2<sup>nd</sup>, 1916 – at Vallarsa our infantry attacked the enemy line stretching from Zugna Torta and Foppiano. Our artillery heavily bombarded the enemy fort at Pozzacchio... along the Posina–Astico frontline we are eventually taking Mount Majo and the south side of Mount Seluggio*».

«*#405, July 3<sup>rd</sup>, 1916 – In the Posina Valley, Italian troops occupied the North–West part of Mount Pruche, Mulini in Val di Zara and Scatolari in the Rio Freddo Valley. Operations are currently underway against the main* *enemy strongholds of this sector at Corno del Coston, Mount Seluggio and Mount Cimone.* »

A bit more realistic and much less focused on war–time propaganda, sounds the official diary of Settimio's Infantry Brigade: «*On July 3rd, the whole 79th Regiment fruitlessly attacked four times the enemy entrenchments... after a few days of rest, our offensive was renewed on July 19th and 20th – this time against Mount Majo. In spite of the outstanding bravery of our soldiers, nothing changed and the overall result proved just as negative and fruitless. On July 24th the Brigade is relieved and sent back in the Colle of Xomo–Mount Ciccheleri sector, to recover from its heavy losses*». From this very source the overall casualties sustained by this infantry Brigade, in the period from May 15th through December 31st, accounted for 11 dead, 84 wounded and 29 M.I.A. officers. Troopers' losses accounted for 367 dead, 3,064 wounded and 1,044 M.I.A.s. Here is a tragic record which luckily will not be repeated in the next years of war.

To better understand the actual holocaust which took place in this sector of the Italian front, a visit to the war cemetery of Arsiero and Schio would definitely help.

In this huge graveyard, thousands of those very infantrymen rest in peace, and on the white tomb stones the 79th is too often engraved. The quiet and humble landscape is sweetly caressed by the light breeze through the cypress trees.

Note: because of the nervous calligraphy, dialect, and grammar, it is impossible to translate Italian to English word for word, but we opted for a very simple and almost literal translation. Ideally, this solution would convey the actual, and untainted meaning and climax of Settimio Damiani's vibrant accounts.

«..... foul smelling meat, days old and a flask of water for each patrol, I got half a cup of it. As soon as we finished lunch we went back to the front line, in the evening the enemy launched a heavy artillery bombardment and many frightened soldiers wanted to run away, but officers commanded them back using their pistols. The artillery deluge lasted about half an hour. I am in the very same spot where some time ago we fought a battle with rifles, grenades and shrapnels. Now the very same battle produces extraordinary

The bombarded ruins of civilian buildings in the Posina Valley, portrayed on a postcard after the Great War. Many of the villagers had left their homes right before the Austro-Hungarian «Punitive Expedition», in 1916. Only in the spring of 1919 the official reconstruction began, but many original and historical buildings had been completely destroyed and thus could not be saved.

The little bridge across the Posina Torrent in the hamlet of La Strenta, near the village of Arsiero.

In the 20s, the Italians buried their troopers along with many Austro-Hungarian soldiers fallen on the surrounding heights, in the very simple military cemetery of Arsiero. It was originally built on the foot of the Redentore Mountain, then moved to the current location - adjacent to the civilian cemetery - by official request of Italian General Giovanni Faracovi, founder of «Onorcaduti» (the Italian Ministry of Defense archive of the fallen soldiers).

One of the most famous Italian newspapers – Corriere Della Sera – on July 21, 1916, reported the major battle raging in the between the Posina Valley sector, between the Italians of Settimio Damiani and the Austro-Hungarian forces. The newspaper included also the official statement given out by the Italian Generalissimo, Luigi Cadorna.

blasts and explosions. The mountain is ablaze, the enemy tried to advance, leaving his trenches, but could not make it. At midnight the battle ceased. On July 13<sup>th</sup> enemy fire was not intense, only a few, random grenades and shrapnel. The height here is 1,175 meters, there are no paths and it's very difficult to transport food along this route. I hope we can be relieved soon. Surprise: on July 2<sup>nd</sup> the battle rages again, at 14:00 a terrible exchange started and lasted 2 hours. Almost 500 Italians were either killed or wounded. The Regiment was now poorly manned. Everybody was pale. Luckily on July 6th the 2<sup>nd</sup> and 3<sup>rd</sup> battalions relieved us. In three days of fighting, the Regiment suffered from more than one thousands casualties, while my company sustained the fewest losses. We thought we were going back to R&R, but once we reached Casa Boara we spent a few days working at supply depots.»

Casa Boaro, located at walking distance from the hamlet of Case Mogentale, was slightly out of reach from the enemy heavy guns and thus used for military stores and depots.

«On July 12<sup>th</sup>, in the morning, our artillery opened up, trying to breach the enemy wire entanglements – they fired back almost as heavily as we did. Many of our guns were put out of action by the enemy's big shells which caused us also some casualties amongst the attendants. Another Austrian big shell hit our mortar gun: it was a real massacre and the entire crew was killed, including the commanding Lieutenant. We were left speechless and in pain in front of the tragedy and such an incredibly precise hit. The enemy artillery kept on pounding us and we could not even move the wounded comrades. A grenade hit a big rock. Such explosions usually scattered rock fragments in all directions, up to a range of 300 meters. I was hit as well in a leg by a flying rock that very day. I was in pain and for the whole day I could not even take a bite. For three days I could barely walk and I would have had the wound checked at the nearest first–aid post, if only it had not been so far away and the Lieutenant had let me go. Later we created a small path to be used for supplies. But, because of the intense artillery fire, for many days nobody could

The Schiri Bridge on the Astico Torrent. This very bridge marked the furthest advance of the Austro-Hungarian troops in the Vicenza sector, during the «Punitive Expedition» of 1916.

A pre-war picture taken at the Borcola Pass, between Mount Pasubio and Mount Maggio. In the distance the cosy village of Griso has not yet been destroyed by the enemy guns. From this village originates the Posina Torrent which runs along the homonymous Valley.

come up and we suffered from thirst and hunger. The grenades kept on exploding all around us, creating deadly storms of rock fragments. The mountain landscape is all upside down and there is no passage, nor path left in this chaos. The lonely, blossoming pine trees are either ablaze or badly scorched by enemy fire. On July 13$^{th}$ we are relieved. We went back some 200 meters to grab a bite in relative peace, after so many tough days. Then we were all assigned with various tasks, including barbed–wire laying and food re-supplying. My platoon has to bury the corpses, but luckily I was spared – my leg is still weak. In the evening the enemy launched another strong attack, our soldiers counterattacked immediately and in few hours they forced the enemy to cease fire. On July 14$^{th}$ one of our shells hit by mistake our front line, killing 3 and wounding 7 men. On the evening of July 14$^{th}$ we were ordered to fake an attack, without leaving the trench. On July 15$^{th}$, my platoon was moved forward and when we reached the advanced position we found some ten foul–smelling corpses – I was ordered to bury them, with the help of 10 brave comrades. They stripped the corpses, removing personal items and cash and then I personally took all these belongings to the administrative officer. I had to wear a protective mask for the unbearable stench of death. Then pouring rain started – everything was drenched and I hung a canvas over my trench for protection, but water was leaking through everywhere, what a torment. All of a sudden a grenade passed over my trench and a shell 305mm. in diameter exploded at some 5 meters from my position: a 10 square meters crater appeared, after the blast. Thank God the shell hit mostly soft ground: I got back on my feet totally covered in soil, but unscathed. At night we were ordered to pack our rain–cloaks and get ready to advance. The first platoon crawled up to the enemy barbed wire, but luckily could not open any breach in it and the attack was halted. All early morning on I suffered from the cold weather – I could not feel my feet any more, it would have been much better to die rather than keep on suffering like this.»

Matching Settimio's entries in his personal diary, the official military reports talked about the abrupt weather changes: «*#418, July 16$^{th}$, 1916 – on the Posina front intense fighting kept on raging in spite of frequent* *thunderstorms which hampered our artillery support. Our troops achieved some territorial gains in the regions of Pasubio, Borcola, Sogli Bianchi, Corno del Coston, Val Dritta, Vanzi and Mount Majo. Strengthened by new reinforcements, the enemy tried to counterattack, but was successfully pushed back and sustained heavy casualties.*»

«On July 16th, massive bombardment of Italian artillery, the enemy responded with heavy caliber deafening grenades. On July 18th, another terrible artillery duel took place. Also the infantry has to advance while all types of shells and bullets scream in the air – guns, mortars, and machine guns. Today more manslaughter will take place, we start the attack. Behind us reinforcements are getting ready. The battle gets worse and worse. Along with my platoon I reached a hill, but its summit is too steep and you cannot stop here, not even if you sit down. The fight does not stop and the platoon commander while right behind us is too scared to come along. All of a sudden the saboteurs' patrol comes back; they could not cut even a single wire in the enemy entanglement. Eventually the fire exchanges stop, but the enemy keeps on bombarding our rear lines. I am some 10 meters away from the enemy's barbed wire; I am a little bit safer than the others, but there is a chance I might be hit by one of our own bullets. On my right there's the 220th infantry Regiment and on the left the 79th.

We cannot dig any entrenchment here as the noise would alert the enemy. We need to talk in whispers. An Austrian patrol could make us prisoners in a jiff. We are too few and no resistance would be possible. Nobody fires a single shot, and since our officers do not really care about us, they remain in the rear. No food can reach us. The cold weather is unbearable and we cannot dig any shelter. Nobody orders to retreat. We were only 15 troopers and 2 officers. Some soldiers were talking about surrendering. «Let's surrender; this is the right time; otherwise everybody dies.» Some would have definitely agreed but that very idea never crossed my mind. A corporal from Friuli said, «Yeah, let's all go to Innsbruck!» (Every Italian soldier used to refer to this Austrian city as the typical location for P.O.W. camps.) The corporal continued: «I know a word or two of Austrian

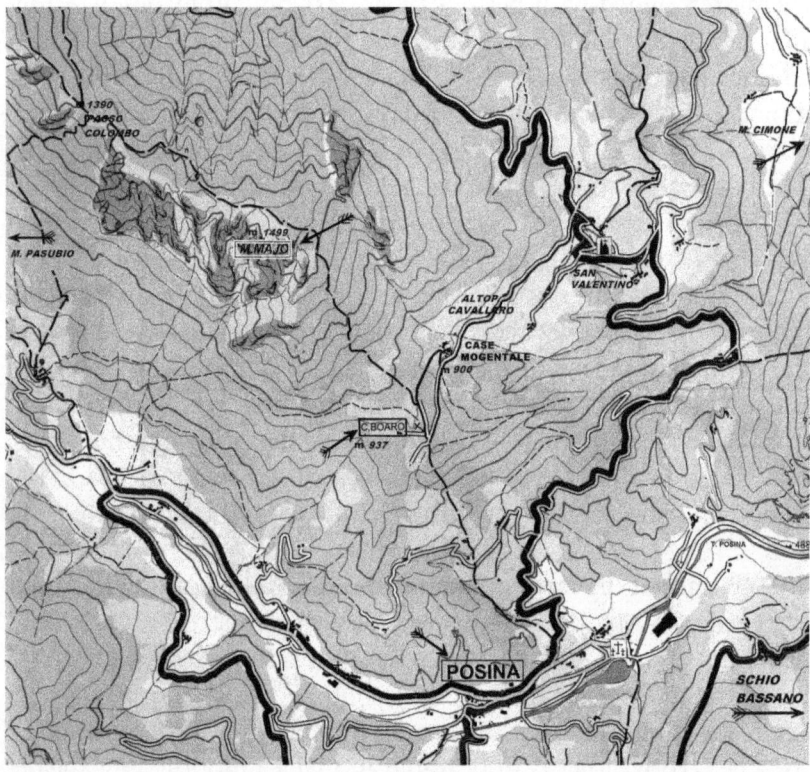

A map of the battle zone in the Posina sector, including the homonymous Torrent and Mount Majo. The Italian Generalissimo – Luigi Cadorna – deployed his troops on the perilous mountain roads across Cogollo del Cengio, Arsiero, Laghi, Posina and Fusine. Appalling quantities of men and war supplies were stacked everywhere in this area. In the spring of 1916 all the local residents were evacuated and Settimio Damiani undoubtedly walked down these very roads with his comrades, carrying his trustworthy «'91» rifle and his backpack. The «Punitive Expedition», launched soon afterwards by the Austro-Hungarians, cost Italy more than 73,000 casualties: twice as many as the enemy's.

# Summer 1916 – In the warzone

A commemorative placard of the «Roma» Brigade with the motto «Sempre più lontano» - «Always further».

A regimental postcard of the «Roma» Brigade bearing the names of its most outstanding battles, the awards received, and its Italian and Latin mottoes. «Col diritto, col sacrificio, col nostro sangue abbiamo preso i nostri confini» - «With our sacrifice and our blood we conquered our borders by full right». «Unde Monita Spes Unde» - «From warnings to hope».

I can go first and then you follow me....» Some soldiers did not like the idea though and eventually we received the order to retreat back to the starting line. We were given some meat and we finally recovered our morale.»

When Damiani talks about the 220$^{th}$ Infantry Regiment he means the «Sele» Brigade Regiment – along with its twin unit, the 219$^{th}$. This Regiment reached the mountains overlooking the city of Schio in May, 1916, tasked with the defense of Mount Novegno. From July 26$^{th}$ through August 1$^{st}$, it was stationed in the first and second lines, with brief rests at the hamlets of Tretto, Piovene, Poleo, Sant'Orso, and Velo. Later on, Damiani will similarly mention the 201$^{st}$ Regiment, meaning the first Regiment of the «Siena» Brigade which was stationed in this sector from Malo and Marano Vicentino, along with its twin Regiment, the 202$^{nd}$ to relieve the «Roma» Brigade.

«On July 20$^{th}$ the weather is very foggy. Each company must nominate two volunteers to bring Bangalore torpedoes up to the enemy barbed wire. Should these explosive devices manage to destroy some wire, a reward will be granted along with some days of rest. Volunteers need to step forward; otherwise each company commander will randomly choose them. It's an order from the Regiment's headquarters. Only one corporal actually volunteered. At night the saboteurs' patrol left for No-man's-land. Some wire was actually destroyed, but soon we heard the enemy promptly repairing it and a second patrol found it back in pristine order.

On July 21$^{st}$, we were relieved by a company of the 20$^{th}$. I was longing to eventually get some rest. We went back to the second line, but we were immediately tasked with resupplies, while all the other companies got some real rest. We are in such misery while stuck on this darn mountain and are continuously pounded by the enemy artillery. Rumours speak about an imminent large offensive. We've been surviving on this darn mountain for some 30 days now and we are just as dirty as real animals. This poor 15$^{th}$ company is cursed and to top it all we've been assigned with a brand new NCO, who is without any particular experience. I was ordered to fetch some barbed wire; other soldiers complain that they are exhausted, but nobody shows any sign of mercy.

On July 22nd the entire company was ordered to bring rations to the 201st Regiment. The enemy is hitting hard on our depots and every now and then we are terrified by the blasts of incredibly powerful shells. Finally, during the night of July 23rd we are dismissed and sent back for rest. We marched all night long, finally reaching the Posina Valley for a brief stop in the morning. Then we proceeded climbing a mountain – I was literally drenched in sweat – eventually reaching a nice, paved road. It looked like a dream. Many of my comrades, totally exhausted, could not proceed any further. Along the way I noticed a small tavern. I flung myself in there like a bird to buy some wine. The owner was obviously sleeping and my comrades and I literally assaulted the tavern owner to wake him up. I was amongst the first customers and I bought a bottle of wine, some canned fruit, chocolate and biscuits – I spent 15 «francs» (Italian Liras). It felt like winning a lottery with all those nice provisions. Then the Lieutenant allowed us to rest for a while and, after a proper lunch, I came back human again. Although I was very tired, I still felt very strong. After another march we stopped in some woods. After lunch we set up a camp with our tents.

On July 26th we received some well deserved praise for the entire company. The 79th suffered many casualties. On July 27th the entire 15th company was ordered to the nearest river for a bath. We hoped also to get some new underwear, but none was distributed. Rumors said: «Tomorrow they want us back in the trenches – they are killing us and if we do not die of misery we'll become the most restless unit in the entire Army! » After 31 days in the trenches, surviving by pure miracle, we were granted only four days of rest. On July 28th, at night, my battalion started marching away, headed for the front lines. Luckily my unit was commanded here and tasked with resupplying chores. My platoon in particular, was ordered to transport barbed wire along with the engineers. During the night of July 29th an entire patrol from the 4th battalion was captured by the enemy although not a single shot was fired. The battalion commander reported them all as deserters. On July 31st my platoon was ordered to a small advanced

Official badge of the 79th Infantry Regiment of the «Roma» Brigade (front). The She-Wolf of the Capitol - «Lupa Capitolina» - feeding the twins Romulus and Remus, is probably the most famous legend and symbol of the city. In the background are the Roman Forum and the Pantheon building. S.P.Q.R. is an initialism from a Latin phrase, «Senatus Popolusque Romanus» - "The Senate and the People of Rome" - referring to the government of the ancient Roman Republic, and used as an official signature of the government. On the top of the badge the number «79» is engraved on the symbol of the «Italian» star.

Official badge of the 79th Infantry Regiment of the «Roma» Brigade (back). An Italian infantryman points at the mountains. On his left, the badge bears the Italian motto of the «Roma» Brigade: «Col diritto, col sacrificio, col nostro sangue abbiamo preso i nostri confini» - «With our sacrifice and our blood we conquered our borders by full right». On the right the Italian royal crown is engraved above the number «79». At the bottom of the badge the Latin motto, «Non fortuna / sed virtute» - «Not by luck, but by virtue».

post. We have to move back and forth to a further advanced line, during every night, without any cover; the enemy could easily spot and capture us. The Lieutenant asked me to keep everybody awake and alert during the night hours. I did not need such order, since I have already been doing so every single night. We could not even cough; we had to keep very still and silent.

At dawn on the third day of August, while I was stepping back from the most advanced post, an Italian sentry, thinking I was an Austrian soldier, fired two shots at me. Luckily the bullets did not hit anybody. I wanted to file a full report blaming it on the one who had allowed all this. The frightened Lieutenant was well hidden away in a nearby cave. If his bosses had known about this, they would have relieved him of his command because he left the troopers alone in front of the enemy for three full days and nights. I have not been sleeping for three days now and food is a mere couple of morsels at night. Luckily now it's quiet. One cannot stand this kind of place for more than three days. Every so often the platoon is relieved.

On August 4th the second platoon is finally relieved from duty. Since we do not have any officer, I kindly asked the Lieutenant to stay with us for another three days. I had a fever, but I could not give up or we must die. I was tired and dizzy, but I had to endure the very same ordeal for another three days in this God forsaken post. On August 6th the third platoon was relieved. I was a dead man walking. I slowly crawled to the starting line and somebody gave me a cup of coffee, some chocolate, cheese, and meat. I got back on my feet and I asked a Lieutenant, who has always been kind to me and whom I've known for some time – ever since I met him in Florence – to let me go and take a rest in some bombarded ruins nearby. He said yes. Three kilometers behind there was a small hut with a light inside. Here I found a soldier cooking potatoes. I had some and then I got some decent sleep. In the morning I felt a bit better.

On August 7th I rejoined my company. During the day I was not assigned any task or chore so I could rest. At night, all the men had to repair trenches, while every now and then we heard the enemy guns in the distance. On August 10th I had a serious fever. The doctor checked me and recorded 102.2 degrees. Hospitalization and paperwork was soon prepared for me. I was sent to a small field hospital at Posina where all the way there I slowly walked with a cane. After a night of sheer terror, the following day a real ambulance took me to the hospital in Schio. Here there were some very nice, real beds and I fell asleep right after putting on some brand new pajamas. I was so happy – it all seemed like a dream.

In the morning I felt much better. After four days in this hospital in Schio, a Red Cross train took me to another hospital in Vicenza. As I was in a real military hospital, I had to go through proper convalescence and therefore I was not given that much food – I was so hungry for ten days! I only got some bread and milk for breakfast, very little soup at lunch, vegetables, a bit of meat, and some bread at dinner. A few minutes after dinner I was already starving again. It was not possible to go outside and buy some bread. Luckily on August 24th I was transferred to the Red Cross hospital at Collegio Albettone. There the food rations improved and there were many nice nurses who kept most kindly reassuring me, telling me that I would get some proper rest after my time at the hospital.»

This picture was taken in the spring on Mount Majo, in 2007. After almost one century, this place, like many other old battlefields in Italy, is still scattered with debris and military items left by the soldiers of the Great War. Many people use metal detectors to retrieve these hidden relics, but it's very easy to find them also without using any particular equipment. The authors of this book were thus able to photograph some cups, rifle cartridges, ration cans and other assorted military items, dating back to the battles of 1915-1918.

Right after the end of the Great War, Italian soldiers gather the bodies of their fallen comrades and offer them properial burial in simple, pinewood coffins.

Imagining the war being over and his grandfather being in a peaceful, serene, and safe place, Dante Damiani, at the age of 22 sketched this impression of Settimio Damiani on his notepad, in California.

# Convalescence with the siena Brigade in Valsugana

As we've seen, on August 10<sup>th</sup>, the health of our hero was threatened by high fever, forcing the field doctor to hospitalize Settimio Damiani in Posina. These days of medical treatment were certainly the best for him during his entire military and war experience.

From the terrible hardship and misery of the trenches, he «escaped» to the dream–like reality of hospital «luxury» with «nice beds and clothes» and «nice and most kind nurses» who could compensate for the scarce rations served.

During the entire Great War, the Vicenza territory looked like an endless rear–front with even the tiniest hamlet turned into barracks and military depots for reserve troops waiting to go back in the front line trenches. Small and medium sized hospitals were scattered everywhere in this region. The Italian historian, Professor De Mori, wrote in his book entitled Vicenza in the Great War, «*Schools and churches, villas, cottages and private buildings were turned into military hospitals which treated thousands of Italian troopers. About 40% of military hospitals in the war zone – which offered some 140,000 beds (plus other 365,000 in the rest of Italy) – were located in the outskirts of Vicenza. Out of the 30,000 beds from 64 Red Cross hospitals in the war zone and 204 scattered all over the Country, ca. 5,000 were available in this very region. Almost 900,000 Italian casualties were treated here over two years of war.*»

«Paradise» did not last that long for Settimio since he was soon discharged from the last hospital and immediately sent back to active duty. This time, he did not rejoin his comrades of the «Roma Brigade» but started wearing the black and yellow insignia of the «Siena.» This unit has already proved a most brave one having taken an active part in 1915 in many major battles on the Carso plateau, and in particular, at San Pietro d'Isonzo, Ronchi, and Castenuovo. In the summer of 1916 the «Siena» Brigade was

The Adrian helmet - "Casque Adrian» in French - was a military helmet issued to the French Army during World War I. It was designed when millions of troops were engaged in trench warfare and head wounds became a significant proportion of battlefield casualties. More than three million Adrians were produced, and they were widely adopted by other countries including Mexico, Italy, Poland, Belgium, Thailand, Russia and Serbia. The helmet in the picture bears the insignia of the «Siena» Infantry Brigade in which Settimio Damiani served, after his hospitalization in 1916.

Italian troopers tasked to resupply units in the field with water.

stationed on Mount Civaron, blocking the Brenta valley. Then in July of the same year, the Brigade helped in capturing Cima Caldiera with a furious attack against the Austrian stronghold on Mount Ortigara which is over the Northern ridge of the Asiago plateau.

It's now September 30$^{th}$, when Settimio Damiani joins the 31$^{st}$ Regiment, 1$^{st}$ battalion, 15$^{th}$ company, facing the Austrian «Schützen» and the Bosnian infantry. The opposing forces were fighting over one of the most spectacular valleys in Italy – Valsugana. This valley is in fact framed on its right by the heights of the Manderiolo, Larici, Portule, Dodici and Ortigara, reaching altitudes of more than 6,500 feet On the right of the Brenta River, the peaks form a less regular line with the even higher crests of Cima d'Asta (9,340 feet), the Lagorai Tower, and Mount Panarotta (9,470 feet).

With heavy snowfall and the harshest temperatures ever recorded, the winter of 1916/17 was probably the coldest of the entire century. Settimio Damiani was going to face this further penitence. The new enemies soon became snow avalanches, blizzards, and frostbites. Many soldiers who died in the heart of winter on these peaks could only be found but would not be given proper burial until late spring. Nonetheless, Damiani seemed to like this portion of the front that was slightly less dangerous than the others.

Settimio arrived at his new trench right after two major blizzards recorded on September 15$^{th}$ and 25$^{th}$ and was grouped with the badly needed reinforcement units.

The «Venezia» Brigade (83$^{rd}$– 84$^{th}$ Regiment) and its twin Regiment, the 32$^{nd}$, shared Settimio's unit's ill-fate in this highly hostile environment.

The official war records speak about the entire 51$^{st}$ Division stationed on the Maora–Brenta sub-sector where No-man's-land was incredibly narrow and opposing forces were almost adjacent to each other. Surely they could not indulge themselves in «local peace agreements» being officially in place, but still it's certain that amongst the opposing forces a mutual «live and let live» attitude was adopted on regular basis. This odd rule of conduct was probably enforced on the troops by the harsh weather conditions themselves.

No major offensive or battle was therefore recorded – only a few skirmishes. Settimio Damiani was soon commanded to lead a re-supply team which had to guarantee the constant and vital flow of food, provisions and war materials to the front line entrenchments. At this point, in spite of his official records, Damiani was very likely promoted to the rank of Corporal, wearing a black, «V»–shaped ribbon on his sleeves. He worked in this sector until February 2nd, 1917, when he was eventually granted some long awaited temporary leave.

«On September 14th I left the hospital, confident about some official leave, but, in spite of my hopes, I was immediately sent to the barracks in Verona. I reached this military camp quite saddened. There I spent four days, got myself some brand new clothes and uniform, took some injections and then I left for Montario, as part of the troops in reserve for the 1st Army. I spent nine days at Montario before the Siena Brigade asked for reinforcements. On September 29th I took a train from Verona and the next day I reached Grigno, Val Sugana. I felt slightly better and a bit relieved, since the Valsugana sector was known as a quiet one. During the night I was assigned to the Regiment and the company and I marched for five hours under pouring rain – when I reach my company I was wet like a fish. I changed my underclothes with some clean and dry ones. I stayed two days at Selva, while the Regiment was waiting for reinforcements. On October 2nd I left for hill 421, in the second line. There was a bombarded house where our platoon was briefly stationed – we could hear the guns roaring and plenty of casualties and wounded soldiers passed by. After a while we were moved to some other huts, closer to the mountains, a place difficult to reach for the enemy shells, while they landed much higher above us. I spent two days here, tasked with re–supplies chores. On October 4th I was commanded to the actual hill 421 in very strongly built trenches, in a tranquil sector. We always worked at night, to further reinforce our defences. In my team there are two guys from Emilia–Romagna region (two «romagnoli») – with them I fetched some boards from nearby bombarded ruins and we built a new trench with this wood.

After 14 days we relieved the third company, currently stationed in the front lines. Luckily the sector was very quiet and I was assigned to a small outpost – the mountain was incredibly steep here and

Settimio Damiani (wearing a white shirt in the photograph) with some comrades. Life in the trenches during the First World War took many forms, and varied widely from sector to sector and from front to front. Undoubtedly, it was entirely unexpected also for those eager thousands of Italians who were enrolled in the army in May 1915.

The village of Valstagna on the foot of the Asiago Plateau, a few kilometres away from Bassano del Grappa. Valstagna was the main depot of the Italian troops which would be deployed on the Asiago Plateau, the Mount Fior-Mount Grappa frontline and the Valsugana Valley. The adjacent river-bed of the Brenta River was amongst the main targets of the Austro-Hungarian offensives during the entire war.

Austro-Hungarian officers photographed behind the front line. Their purposely polished uniforms and forced smiles were the best way to spare their relatives the horror of the daily onslaughts of a terrible war of attrition.

they had to bring us lunch with an elevator [Settimio is referring to cableways, often used for these purposes by both armies]. From my position I could clearly see the Austrians working and gathering around bonfires, but they did not shoot at us and we simply did the same – no officer came to supervise or check our activities, since we were stationed in a very hazardous position. Fourteen days passed by without a single casualty. At night my feet suffered from the bitter cold, but we fought the low temperature by getting together, staying very close to each other.

Food always reached us very cold as well and we had to warm it up with the food heaters in our trench. On October 20$^{th}$ our platoon was relieved and I got back to the second lines, tasked again with re-supply chores. Here life was a bit better and I was spared the task of carrying the heavy canteens and food containers. Officers are spared from these chores in this Regiment [as previously mentioned, at this point Settimio must have been promoted to the rank of Corporal for sure]. Every time I had to lead my team, I was forced to shout and yell in order to find and gather all my men – nobody was particularly eager to walk for 2 or 3 kilometers on a steep climb, burdened by 30 kilograms of food – every fifty paces or so, we had to stop, but no matter how tired the men got, we had to proceed, even under the pouring rain on a slippery and thus very dangerous track. Some soldiers invoked death, they screamed: «It's better to die right here and right now, rather than suffer like this!» Eventually, on November 16$^{th}$ the long awaited 32$^{nd}$ Regiment came to relieve us.

We marched all the way back to the rear lines, with a brief stop at dawn in the hamlet of Selva – the enemy guns were already very far away. I felt relieved, had some coffee and food and at eight o'clock we proceeded to Tezze. After 45 days in the war zone we saw some civilians again – I was exhilarated. It looked like a totally different world. There I found also an inn-keeper who sold me wine, canned fruit and chocolate.»

Tezze is a small village, on the left of the Brenta River, between Primolano and Grigno. Nowadays Fastro is partially under the Arsie' jurisdiction (Belluno) and partially in the territory of Cismon del Grappa

(Vicenza). In this little town there was a small barrack of the «Finanzieri» (Customs/Borders officers), tasked with the protection of the border ever since the beginning of the century.

«After 15 minutes of rest we started marching again. Our journey lasted 24 hours and in the evening of November $17^{th}$ we reached Fastro, incredibly weary and tired. Since many soldiers could not march any longer, everybody was put in private homes and given some hay for makeshift beds. I slept very well, in a very nice room, along with my team. Then we found another private home where six of us stayed for one month – the family was very friendly. I seldom used my canteen to eat. I spent three or four francs a day shopping for food. I ate incredibly well and I did not really care about money. Every day I could buy maccheroni pasta, eggs, meat, sometimes chicken. I prayed to spend the forthcoming Christmas season in this nice hamlet, but after 32 days we had to go back to the war zone. On December $17^{th}$ we left and during the first stop in Grigno we heard the enemy guns roaring again in the distance. The entire platoon spent one night inside some bombarded ruins. On the $18^{th}$, the first company moved to the huge trench at Ospedaletto. We marched along a camouflaged road, keeping a good distance between us, while enemy grenades and shrapnel – exploding twice – kept on searching for us. The enemy was well aware of our movements on that road.»

The shells «exploding twice» which Settimio talks about were one of the three types of projectiles available to the Austrian Army. The shells were actual grenades, packed with fragments of metal (shrapnel). Upon impacting the ground, the main shell blasted out the shrapnel container, which then exploded its own charge, producing a storm of lethal bullets.

«I reached the huge trench and I saw that, in spite of many enemy shells landing on it, it cannot be so easily hit or destroyed. Inside the trench there is plenty of slits for rifles and machine guns, along with shelters and small dug-out. Also this portion of the front is pretty calm. Any kind of push or advance is out of the question here: the mountains are impervious. Every day we work to reinforce the

Settimio Damiani portrayed in a rare photograph during the war. In the 20s, the Italian infantryman was awarded two commemorative medals for the veterans of the Great War. In spite of his many tremendous responsibilities during the war, Settimio Damiani was never promoted even to the rank of Corporal in the Italian Army.

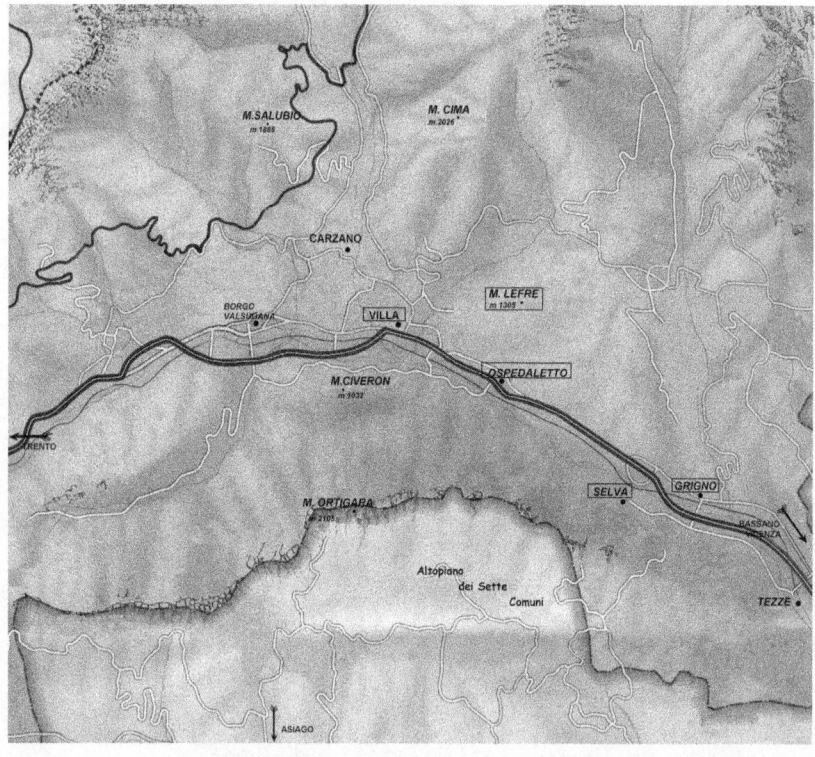

A map of the Valsugana Valley. Fierce battles took place in and around the villages of Ospedaletto, Selza, Tezze, Borgo, Villa and Grigno in one of the most spectacular Italian valleys which stretches between the regions of Trentino and Veneto. On the right of the Valsugana Valley many surrounding heights were similarly involved in major clashes between the Italian and the Austro-Hungarian armies. Mount Manderiolo, Mount Larici, Mount Portule, Cima Dodici and Mount Ortigara were, in fact, bathed in the blood of thousands of young soldiers during the Great War.

Convalescence with the siena Brigade in Valsugana 69

Italian soldiers wearing primitve gas masks in the trenches. Early gas masks were crude as would be expected as no-one had thought that poison gas would ever be used in warfare as the mere thought seemed too shocking. This crude masks gave proved to be very weak and easy to break - thus making their protective value null and void. The masks gave protection by being dipped in anti-gas chemicals or even simple urine.

The graves of two infrantrymen of the "Roma" Brigade in which Settimio Damiani served in 1916. This fallen soldiers rest in the military cemetery of Arsiero, near Vicenza, with hundreds of other Italian troopers of the Great War. Where nowadays many attractive tourist resorts can be found a few miles away from the industrial city of Vicenza, there used to be many depots and concentration area for the Italian soldiers.

trench and we move huge quantities of barbed wire. The Valsugana appears completely plastered with barbed wire. Sometimes I must take part in night patrols and on Christmas Eve I almost reached the enemy entanglements. When baby Jesus was born I could clearly hear Austrian soldiers praying and ringing a small bell – I was relieved, since I was sure there would have been no gun fight that night, in fact not a single shot was fired. Only some Very Lights and a huge searchlight sweeping No-man's-land. When the latter hit my position I laid flat on my belly, keeping very still. On New Year's Eve I was once again in No-man's-land, positioning barbed wire. I heard the Austrians talking, while they exploded some coloured flares and exchanged greetings at midnight. In the small hamlet of Ospitaletto there was a little inn where, from time to time, I went to buy wine and canned sardines. On January 6th, at night, while almost freezing under the moonlight, I had some good times with my comrades, sardines and wine – the front was very calm and we were pretty happy.»

Since summer 1916 in this sector of the Val Sugana many Italian soldiers fought and were replaced on regular basis. The 10th division left for the Isonzo front and this sector had to be protected by the «Campania» Brigade (135th and 136th infantry Regiment), the 31st Regiment of the Brigade «Siena», the 13th Brigade of the Territorials and the artillery units formerly assigned to the 10th division. All these units were grouped in the 51st division and led by general Cossu. The troops were deployed from Mount Lefre, on the left of the Valsugana, to Cima Caldiera, on the Northern ridge of the Asiago plateau.

On the Austrian side, the special «Valsugana Group» has been created. It was deployed from Passo dell'Agnella, right behind the summit of Mount Ortigara, to the area where Calamento valley meets Campelle Valley. Ten battalions of regular troops and five units of «Standschützen» formed the 18th Imperial division, led by field–marshal Edl von Scholz. Further northeast, towards the Lagorai mountains and well over this peak, was stationed the right wing of the XXth Army corps that had been recently created by the newly–appointed, Austrian Emperor, Charles. Franz Joseph had passed away on November 22nd, 1916.

# Campaign of 1917

In the spring of 1917 the «suicide of Europe» which shed blood all over the continent, had been enforcing terrible and recurrent manslaughter on the Armies of all the powers involved. No way out from the stall of trench war was in sight and no «easy victory» or strategic advance could be achieved. The generals shared the very same low morale of their troops imprisoned in the misery of the trenches while waiting for the next suicidal attack. Many deserters were reported, along with many self-inflicted wounds and mutinies. Furthermore, a large number of young men drafted for military service, ran away or hid from the recruiting patrol of «Carabinieri» – the military police. Court Martials were very strict and firing squads killed not only the men but the overall morale of the fighting troops.

The Italian front was shaped like a big «S», lying horizontally. Where it protruded in the Trentino salient, Luigi Cadorna, the Italian Generalissimo, had to adopt defensive attitudes, while the main aggressive thrust was focused further North on the Isonzo river and the Carso plateau. On this part of the front, Cadorna adopted his infamous strategy of the «big pushes», the so-called «Spallate» – «Shoulder hits», fighting a real war of materials. Any deeper and more comprehensive idea of a strategy was a concept completely unknown to the mind of this general and unknown to all the other Great War commanders as well.

«On January 15$^{th}$ we move to the front line, snow fell all night long. We marched in more than 40 inches of snow. No track was visible, and with a very heavy backpack I reached the advance line completely exhausted. I had to shovel the snow away along with my team. The fourth team was attached to the 83$^{rd}$ infantry Regiment. On January 17$^{th}$ we suffered from an avalanche and 32 soldiers were buried alive – we managed to rescue only two, badly wounded. All night long

Official badge of the 31st and 32nd Infantry Regiments of the «Siena» Brigade. Settimio Damiani was serving in this very unit when he was captured by Austro-German forces during the Battle of Caporetto. This bronze badge bears the She-Wolf of the Capitol - «Lupa Capitolina», Latin motto «Sena vetus virtus nova» - «Old Siena, New Courage» and the Italian dedication to this Infantry Brigade.

One of the many temporary military cemeteries built during the Great War on the Venetian plains. At the end of the conflict all the soldiers buried in these locations were transferred to much bigger, permanent shrines built in Arsiero, Asiago, Valli del Pasubio, Schio and on Mount Cimone.

we had to move and position barbed wire with incredible misery and every now and then terrifying enemy grenades impacted all around us. Every four days the platoon was relieved. I went to Ivano, a small bombarded hamlet nearby. The cold was simply unbearable and many soldiers had to be hospitalized because of frostbites in their feet.»

Ivano–Fracena, located at an altitude of 1,500 feet, is a tiny village on the northern foot of Mount Lefre – this mountain dominates the whole Vasugana, reaching the height of 4,280 feet.

«On January 25$^{th}$, my platoon was transported into some barracks on Mount Lefre. It was a nice spot, although the enemy, one kilometer in front of us, kept on bombarding our rear lines. On February 2$^{nd}$ I received the long-awaited winter leave, I was overwhelmed by sheer joy. I took my backpack and reached battalion HQ – there I received all the official papers and I proceeded straight to Grigno, to the Brigade HQ. I left all my gear there and then I proceeded to Trezze.

In March I arrived at Istrana, near Treviso. I spent a month there, re-training and taking some more shots for cholera and typhus.»

The «Siena» Brigade left this sector at the end of March and was replaced by the 17$^{th}$ e 18$^{th}$ Regiments of the «Bersaglieri» Brigade and deployed on the very same line between the northern ridge of the Asiago plateaus and Mount Lefre. The horrible and endless manslaughter of the Carso plateau kept asking for more and more young blood.

# The tenth battle of the Isonzo

In May 1917, Settimio Damiani, now belonging to the 31$^{st}$ infantry Regiment of the «Siena» Brigade, was transferred to Cervignano, in the southern portion of the Carso plateau, amongst the main war-zones. Here, operated the 3$^{rd}$ Italian Army, led by the Duke of Aosta.

Luigi Cadorna was preparing his tenth major push for some months and now was eager to launch the attack which ideally should have opened the way to Trieste. The battle had to begin with intense artillery bombardment – possibly the most devastating of the whole war – followed by a particular maneuver of the 2$^{nd}$ Army of general Luigi Capello to fight against the enemy positions on the Bainsizza plateau and around the city of Gorizia. Then a major thrust was to be launched towards Trieste by the 3$^{rd}$ Army of the Duke of Aosta. The entire Italian Army was 308 infantry battalions strong, with 2,238 guns and 986 mortars – an impressive and unbeatable display of forces, much bigger than the scarce and worn-out resources of the 5$^{th}$ Army of Austro-Hungarian general Boroevič.

The first phase of the offensive, the one assigned to the 2$^{nd}$ Army, would have also laid the very first strategic brick of the forthcoming last battle of the Isonzo eventually leading to the conquest of the Bainsizza plateau. This would have also meant a very dangerous and too advanced positioning of general Capello's forces; oddly, during the infamous Caporetto rout, the enemy profited from this.

The «butcher of the Isonzo», as Capello was also known, considered his secondary role in the tenth battle as the perfect opportunity to forge the brand new soldiers of Italy, exclusively «armed» with courage and indomitable willpower against the impenetrable machine-gun nests of the enemy! Emanuele Filiberto, the Duke of Aosta, was much more realistic; without hoping for any miracle, he simply followed his order.

The foot of Mount Brestovi seen from the village of Doberdò.

At dawn, on May 12$^{th}$ 1917, at dawn, 2,150 Italian guns erupted against the Austro–Hungarians, pounding every single enemy position for two full days until May 14$^{th}$. Thousands of casualties were inflicted upon the opposing forces, destroying outposts, trenches and depots.

At noon, on May 14$^{th}$, the II$^{nd}$ Corps, led by the newly–appointed general Pietro Badoglio, launched its attack against Hill 383, on the Bainsizza plateau. After a full week of fighting, 30,000 casualties were suffered by the enemy, but this figure could not even compare to the Italian dead and wounded. Cadorna, nonetheless, was able to conquer the bridge–heads of Plava and Mount Kuk and the heights of the Vodice hill; ten major manslaughters, including this terrible battle, had been fought for these very minor objectives. Now, the 3$^{rd}$ Army was ready to do its part in attacking the Carso region which would then lead to Trieste. In his diary, Settimio Damiani recorded the terrifying experience of the initial artillery bombardment on May 23$^{rd}$. This very event was also referred to as the «one hundred–thousand grenade per hour» battle. At 4 p.m. of the same day, the guns of the Duke of Aosta accounted for more than 1 million shells launched which amounted to an average of 20 projectiles every 12 inches of land.

The Austro–Hungarian defenders on the very first lines were totally annihilated and the few survivors had to fight to death without any reinforcement available. Six divisions of the VII$^{th}$ and XXIII$^{rd}$ Army groups of the «Isonzoarmee» (the Army of the Isonzo) were thus lost. A strong wind blew against the carefully calculated trajectories of many lighter shells, thus jeopardizing the main goal of breaching the dense wire entanglements across No-man's-land. Siege mortar projectiles backfired on their own attendants, again because of the strong gale. Eventually, the Italian infantry was launched, but their progress was sensibly hampered by such partly faulty artillery preparation.

The troopers of the Duke of Aosta challenged every possible obstacle and quickly reached and took the enemy rear lines, up to the large valley («Vallone») in front of Selo, quite often mentioned in the diary.

«In May we moved to the new front and arrived at Cervignano on the 9$^{th}$. I immediately noticed intense movements in this sector and I correctly guessed that we would have been later stationed on the Carso plateau. In Cervignano we set up tents and spent twenty days. Every night enemy airplanes came to bomb Cervignano and Villa Vicentina: the blasts of their cargoes kept us awake all night long. To top it all, Austrian naval guns kept on bombing us from the nearby gulf. On May 20[th] we receive the order to get ready to move. At night we start marching, while rumors mentioned an imminent major attack, scheduled for the 23[rd]. It seemed like we had to be part of it. On the night of the 21[st] we slept out in the open, waiting to go to the front lines. On the 22[nd] the Major in command of our battalion read us the latest official bulletin: Our comrades on the Carso plateau just captured some 2000 prisoners. We must get ourselves ready! Therefore we have to be part of the action. On the very same day we were ordered to leave all our backpacks, while keeping our battle gear. On the 23[rd] the first battalion started marching from Ferleti; ever since May 22[nd] we could hear our guns at work, every route, road and path were clustered with transports and troops; it was almost impossible to proceed.»

The «Siena» Brigade was now under the 33[rd] division in the Ferleti sector and the Tenth Battle of the Isonzo was already well underway when Damiani reached Doberdò, during the night of May 23[rd]. The «Siena» and the I[st] and II[nd] grenadiers Regiments were the actual troops which started marching towards the front line. On May 25[th], after many bloody exchanges and while insignificant hills kept on changing hand, the grenadiers were halted and ordered to entrench themselves. At this point, they were also being relieved, in the last useless attack, by the very men of the «Siena.» After some 24 hours of relative calm, Settimio Damiani and his comrades attacked the enemy, suffering hundreds of casualties with zero results.

«On May 24[th] I arrived in the Vallone of Iamiano. The bombardment never ceased; we saw many prisoners coming down from the hills; they were shell–shocked and asked for food. As soon as we reached the Vallone, coffee and hand–grenades were distributed. Today an enemy airplane was shot down by one of ours: everybody cheered and clapped hands. During the afternoon march toward the front lines a shrapnel hit my team commander in a leg. Everybody would have welcomed such a «smart» wound. Why I could not get

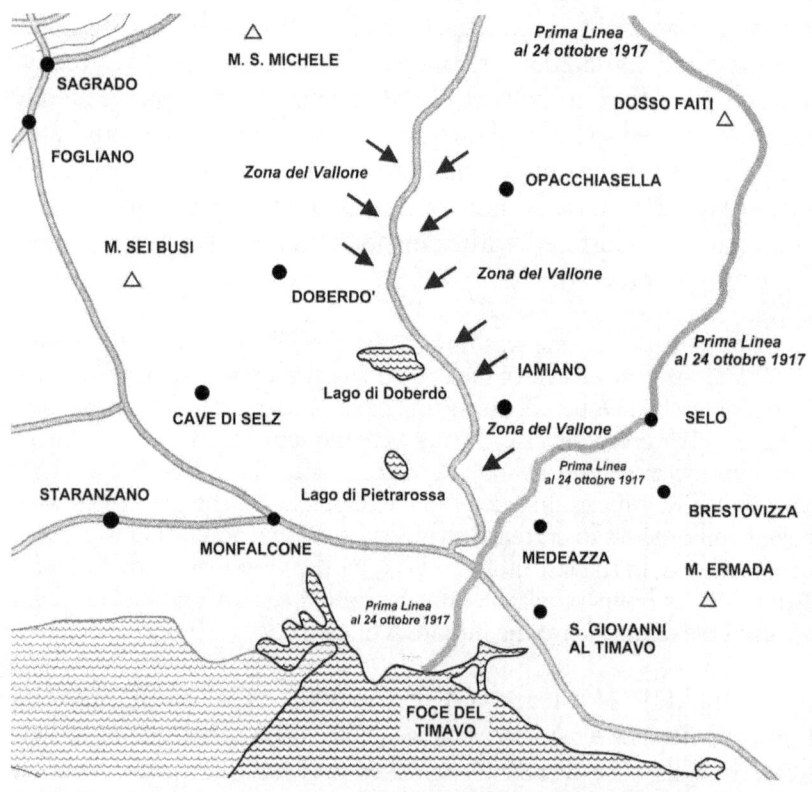

A detailed map of the Doberdò sector where the Tenth and the Eleventh Battle of the Isonzo took place, in the summer of 1917. Settimio Damiani was actively involved in both.

one myself? I had to take command of the team, although I would have preferred not.»

Also during the following day, May 25th, ferocious fighting took place on the southern ridge of the Carso plateau. Attacks were followed by counterattacks and the troops on both sides were exhausted. Italians and «Frontkämpfer» could not achieve any real success. On May 26th, Settimio Damiani took part to some minor exchanges and by dawn of the following day the battle was definitely over. Local guerrilla raged on though, as reported in the diary of Settimio Damiani.

On the second anniversary of the beginning of the war, the VII Corp of general Tettoni, recorded the most significant results in the entire maneuver. It took two major enemy strongholds, taking 9.000 prisoners – the very same men Damiani saw shell–shocked and hungry in the Italian rear lines. During the first hours of May 24th the 7th also the Austro–Hungarian division looked for some glory, trying to repel the attacks of the Italian XIII Corps from the area around Selo. But Settimio Damiani's men were still strong enough and motivated to resist and then successfully counterattack the enemy thrust; some 5,000 casualties were reported just amongst the Austro–Hungarian frontline riflemen. Our protagonist was tasked mainly with re–supplying chores and these details help us understand the total chaos he describes along with some information about officially reported fights. When Damiani talks about stretcher–bearers, wounded soldiers and corpses scattered all over the battlefield, he sadly reminds us of some verses of Italian poet Gabriele D'Annunzio's poem «Doberdo' Prayer»: *«Kneeling down they cuddle their own pain or simply stare at it, laying on an arm or an elbow, or with their heads between their knees, with childish smiles plastered forever on dry mouths or with the maelstrom of the battle frozen in their eyes.»*

«As soon as I reached the foot of the hill with my company, I was ordered to transport ammunition under never–ceasing artillery fire and along very shallow trenches. It was impossible to walk. We had make to room for a constant flow of wounded soldiers and stretcher–bearers, while our feet slipped over human bodies, fallen dead inside the trench. It is not possible to even peek over the parapet. It's a real terror: the stench of the dead is unbearable. I did not believe that the Carso could be such a bloody battlefield. Our offensive continues. On May 26th, my battalion moved to the starting line of attack. During this march we had to actually run in a certain area, because the enemy was pounding us with shells without stopping – there are also many shells with asphyxiating gas. Many comrades, dead inside the trenches, turned yellowish because of sulphur gas. On May 27th, in full daylight, the 2nd and 3rd advanced with their teams very close to each other. The enemy spotted the movement and counterattacked with a terrible battle. All over the hills shells are raining down; our battalion is standing by on reserve; we cannot see much because of dense smoke, we cannot tell the earth from the sky, our artillery respond with equal density of shell. Some grenades hit very near. The blasts are terrifying. At night the news says that the two battalions suffered many casualties and could not advance. On the 28th my battalion advanced at Iamiano. We reached a hill [either one of the two in this area, Hill 192 or Hill 175] during the night. We were ordered to stop and set up a camp. The Major leading us is hit and command goes to a Captain [according to official records, Major Vincenzo Vergara was hit during combat and thus relieved in command by Captain Antonio Salvio].

After an hour's stop, we restarted the advance, in scattered teams. The enemy, alerted by our movement, launch volleys of barrage with its artillery. Our marching orders are no more valid, everybody has to run for cover. The officers... «Let's move! Attack! Forward!» Daylight appears and we must advance anyway, very sad and worried – with its thousands of guns the enemy is launching the fire of hell against our poor battalion. Today everybody dies, there is not a single square foot of ground without a corpse; it's sheer terror. I can see every type of dead soldier, while wounded cry and scream but cannot be rescued as long as the battle rages on. Grenades keep on exploding, covering me with soil; I became all black and I spit black, death passes often in front of my eyes. The captain calls for help; he too has been hit. Amongst smoke and cannonades we cannot see anything. Everybody wanders on his own. I luckily found a cavern dug by the Austrians and I found

The Italian front line near the Doberdò Lake. The soldier in the picture is burdened by special containers full of water, a priceless commodity on such a barren and sun-scorched landscape.

shelter inside. Here I found two soldier of the third battalion. I took a breath. One soldier had some chocolate of his lieutenant with him and shared it with me. Thirst is killing us; nobody had a single drop of water. Luckily a rain cloud passed by and I use my canteen to get some drops of black water. It tasted bitter, but I did not care. As soon as night came, I left the cavern and re–joined my company. I walked for an hour and then I found my sergeant–major, very sad, with four soldiers inside a cavern; he could not speak. Many wounded are inside the cavern and they cried for help, but nobody had enough strength left to take them away. Everybody was screaming for food, so I shared some canned meat from my backpack. I asked where the rest of the company was, but nobody knew; everybody was completely lost. All of a sudden, under the rock I saw the lieutenants of my company, Martoni and Lapilli, screaming for help; one of them is wounded. During the night, captain Valini from the 5[th] company arrives, [it's actually Ettore Valino and not Valini], gathers the soldiers, and takes command of the battalion, leading us up to the line occupied by the 234[th] infantry Regiment. On the morning of May 30[th], a lieutenant gave orders to two teams to go fetch some food and water, since everybody was starving and suffering particularly from thirst; we sighed. The rations teams did not came back until night – maybe they have been hit or found refuge or shelter. Every path and every trench are turned upside down, completely in chaos and terror is everywhere. A soldier from the 234[th] Regiment eventually brought us a canteen filled with water. All the soldiers run to him, with their tin cups, hoping to get at least a few drops. But to us, from the 31[st] Regiment, no water was given at all. A soldier from my company fell to the ground, dying of thirst. Stretcher–bearers arrived and put him on a stretcher, the military priest arrived as well and gave him some water and liquor, but the soldier does not speak anymore; they take him away. The good chaplain looks at us and gives a single drink of water to everybody.»

For the Italian soldiers, attacking on the Carso plateau, dehydration was the most dangerous risk. During the preparation of the Tenth Battle of the Isonzo, no strategist, nor any commander ever considered the vital need of re–supplying their troops with water during each attack. The similar,

An Italian howitzer, fondly known as 'hippopotamus', being set up on the Isonzo River battlefield. The gun is surrounded by soldiers, most of whom appear to be involved in the preparation work. There appears to be a pulley or lifting mechanism to the right, possibly for moving the large shells into position. To keep up with the stride of artillery development during the Great War, it was found advisable to design bigger and bigger howitzers with longer range.

An Italian sentry observes the effects of an intense bombardment of the enemy lines across the Doberdò Plateau. The Doberdò plateau was in fact crossed by the main front line and on the very area of exceptionally intense battles that were fought between August 1916, through May 1917, when the Italians reached the village of Iamiano, east of Doberdò. In the wide valley, often mentioned by Settimio Damiani, there were endless Italian depots, huts and barracks, and even small, military cemeteries

tragic episode of the Dardanelles, in 1915, occurred when the British troops were stranded, on barren and sun-scorched terrain, without a single drop of water, but the Italians seemed to ignore the lesson. The «lunar» Carsic landscape, in fact, proved just as dry as the Gallipoli peninsula's coastline and the hot summer of 1917 literally turned it into a hellish furnace; the landscape having no spring nor reservoir in sight. A soldier could have kept going for days without food, but it only took few hours to drive him mad without at least a sip of water. Many even tried to drink their own urine, desperately looking for some liquid. As we previously mentioned, Settimio Damiani, enlisted in the $31^{st}$ Regiment of the Siena Brigade, was engaged in the front as well as in the rear lines, mostly moving and transporting military supplies and tons of barbed wire. Also, according to the official records, they mention the support role of the entire $21^{st}$ division, made of the Siena and the Pistoia Brigades, up to the month of September 1917. At the end of the offensive, the Italians had suffered 160,000 casualties, about 60% of the whole Army. A similar figure was enforced on the enemy. To make things even worse, the Austrians had captured about 3000 prisoners more than the Italians – a clear symptom of the dramatically decreased energy and fighting spirit of the Italians. In fact, Damiani reports many episodes of desertion which quickly led the firing squads.

«On June $1^{st}$, as nobody sent for provisions has yet come back, the captain called me, sigh! «Come on Damiani, do me a favor, take three or four soldiers and go to the field kitchens for food. And make sure you come back!»

«I will do my very best, sir!» I said and with four comrades I started running, while the enemy was furiously shooting, we did not think about the bullets, instead we focused on our hunger and thirst which were really unbearable. Luckily, after walking through so many paths and trenches we found the kitchens and we rested for a while. The cooks gave us a half cup of coffee and bread and I made a nice soup. We got some strength back and then the commanding lieutenant give us canned meat, two bags of bread and two containers full of water. I started my way back. We soon got lost, with so many different paths and trails. Nobody could tell us the right way to reach my Regiment, not even the command post of the $17^{th}$ infantry Regiment. I walked on, through some more trenches where there was every type

Italian troops marching towards Iamiano, on the eastern ridge of the Doberdò Plateau. This very ridge was eventually conquered by the Italians only after two full years of war and horrifying numbers of casualties - the actual territorial gain accounted for only a few kilometres, in spite of the never-ending onslaughts.

The small lake on the Doberdò Plateau. Behind the hills in the backgrounds is the city of Monfalcone and the Adriatic Sea.

of corpse; in some places I could see even four or five of them piled up. The enemy was also merciless shooting many stretcher-bearers, even when they clearly had shown the Red Cross symbol. I stopped in a cavern and there I found five wounded Austrians... prisoners with nobody in sight to lead them away. After a brief stop, I walked away and night came; we've been walking all day long. I saw the command post of the 234$^{th}$ Regiment. A lieutenant sent us a guide, so I took heart again. Eventually I reached my company and upon seeing us, everybody cheered and smiled. Everybody gathered around us, holding their tin cups, more thirsty than hungry. The sergeant major arrived and distributed half a cup of water, a can of meat, and half bread loaf. The captain wanted to know where had the previous teams gone. They were all lost in the chaos – scared, terrified, and did not dare to advance any further. I saw thousands of men from various Regiments, all scared to death and exhausted.»

«On June 2$^{nd}$, the 14$^{th}$ Battalion from the 31$^{st}$ Regiment was ordered to form a new line, connected to the 234$^{th}$ infantry Regiment. Eventually, at night, some men brought us more food, bread, coffee and lemons; we took heart again. Later, we were ordered to retire, back to the starting line. The whole battalion is a mere 200 men strong and, while we retreated, many skirters came out from their hideouts and joined our march. When we arrived on the starting line some more food was distributed. We had a nice dinner with food, wine, coffee and Marsala wine. The captain in charge of the battalion, asked, «How are you doing guys?!»

Many were laughing at us while nobody was looking, saying that anybody actually fighting in such carnage was really stupid. Me and four comrades found a nice cavern. After eating I fell asleep; my eyes were tired with sleep; I have not been sleeping for many days. While I was asleep another order came, «Wake up boys, get your capes and backpacks, we are going to form a new line!»

As soon as we arrived on our new positions, every 3 or 4 men had to build new trenches with rocks. On July 3$^{rd}$ the enemy desperately counterattacked again, the guns were vomiting fire and from both sides came a deluge of shells.»

On the Carso plateau it was not possible to dig very deep trenches; therefore most of the parapets were built with stones and rock fragments which were available in large quantities. This, unfortunately, increased the effectiveness of enemy shells which, upon exploding, scattered hails of rock splinters and fragments all over the impact area. The very same materials used to protect the Italians, thus turned in lethal shrapnel.

«Today we cannot survive. The rock splinters make a non–stopping rain, many soldiers run away form the front line trenches, crying and saying that the enemy is rapidly advancing, furiously firing at us. Many soldiers of my very same age from the 140th Regiment run away so quickly that they even dropped their guns. The Austrians advanced with many platoons side by side. We cannot stand the bombardment; the Carsic hills are ablaze. Many prisoners told us that the Austrians have moved troops from the Russian front and brought them here to massively counterattack. In fact, a terrible battle like this has never been seen before. Some guns launch incredibly powerful shells that scare you to death upon exploding.»

At 2:00 o'clock on June 4th, infantrymen of the 140th and 139th Regiment (Bari Brigade) and two units from the 2nd battalion of the 31st Regiment (Siena Brigade) attacked and re–took all the positions on hill 241, except its very top, which was lost the day before. For the Italians, badly bruised, battered and worn–out, the Austrian counterattack came as another death sentence. All the units, urgently commanded to stop the counterattack – the Siena Brigade and the Ist and IInd Grenadiers Regiments amongst them – fought desperately and most bravely. On the morning of June 6th, the Ist Grenadiers Regiment was once again ordered into the battle, and supported by the men of the Siena Brigade, had to take Hill 219 and Hill 235 in the Fornaza area. This desperate goal was achieved with further impressive casualties.

«On June 4th, 1917, the fighting got tougher and tougher. The screams of the wounded can be heard everywhere. Luckily, at night came the order to retreat. Again, we got back to the starting line. On the 5th came the order to advance once more. Me and twenty soldiers were ordered to transport the wounded of the Sardinia Brigade

This picture was taken in the public parking lot near the lake of Doberdò, facing east. The little building in the distance is «Casa Cadorna» - «The House of Cadorna». The hill is part of the «vallone» area often described in details in the diary of Settimio Damiani.

This picture, taken in Selo (Slovenia), shows the eastern face of Mount Selo. This minor height is the opposite ridge of the «vallone» - «the big valley» - where Settimio Damiani fought in the summer of 1917 and nowadays is well inside the Slovenian border.

[Grenadiers of Sardegna]. I left with these soldiers and fetched 10 stretchers. The captain of this unit wrote down my name and told me: «If you do not come back with the wounded tonight, I will report you as a deserter.»
Before leaving I went to the field kitchen for some comfort. Then I left with my team; it was a continuous bombardment with shrapnel. The enemy knew about our continuous movement at night and kept on searching the whole battlefield with its spotlights. All of a sudden while crossing a narrow path, a hail of bullets and shrapnel went through my legs. I do not know how I could save myself. A soldier from my team screamed and he was hit. We arrived very tired at the line kept by the grenadiers; many of my men could not come and were scared. The trenches were filled with corpses, and bullets of all kind whistled in the air. I arrived at the 21st Regiment exhausted. Inside a gallery there were many wounded, screaming in pain. It was terrible to hear their pain. The captain doctor congratulated me himself, about facing such a danger; there were four soldiers seriously wounded and a slightly wounded one. Around midnight we left the cavern with the wounded men, while walking on improvised paths. Luckily the bombardment had ceased. When I reached a small hamlet we rested for a short while. Everything had been bombarded and destroyed – ruins were everywhere. I arrived at the first aid post and there I left the wounded to be taken away. My battalion had already left for the advanced line, so I found shelter inside a cavern. My team rested all night, and from the lines came the news: «The Sardegna Brigade blocked the Austrian counter–attack! The Austrians were advancing with many companies side by side.» The Siena Brigade has been working on these terrible hills for fifteen days now, and nobody is yet relieving it, while the Ancona Brigade was replaced after only two days. On June 6th, eventually those poor grenadiers came to relieve us. They had only two days of rest.

I took some bread and coffee. I was very pale and could not speak. The few soldiers with me wandered without command, officers were very few and we walked like disoriented sheep. I had grown such a rough beard that nobody would have recognized me; we stared at each other in the middle of the carnage....everywhere. As soon as I reached San Pier d'Isonzo, the local host gave me half a liter of vermouth and I took some heart. Then I walked on until I reached a small pinewood where I found the rest of my Regiment. In a nearby village I was able to cash two wires I received while I was in the trenches – one from America and one from mom. I immediately went to the wine cellar and thought that I was alive thanks to a miracle. I bought a backpack of stuff, including Marsala wine, wine, biscuits and canned fruit. I spent 25 liras. Then I got back to my company to eat and drink and I got a bit drunk. Then I took a nap under a pine tree, amongst the rocks in the open air. I fell asleep so nicely that I slept for the entire night.

On June 7$^{th}$ a caravan of trucks came to take the whole Regiment away to some proper R&R.

After 40 Km., we stopped for five days inside some huts. We finally changed our clothes and became human again. On July 14$^{th}$ we were transferred again; this time by marching and stopping twice to rest. Then we reached a village [Polazzo] where we stayed for fifteen days of R&R. After so many days under such terrible bombardments, here I spent some joyful time. I slept very well and I could not hear the roaring guns anymore. On July 2$^{nd}$ we marched for some more 20 Kilometers; then we set up camp and spent an other eight days of R&R in the village of Doberdò. On July 10$^{th}$, quite unexpectedly, arrived the order to get ourselves prepared to move back to the frontlines again.»

During the entire war all the buildings of the village of Doberdò were bombarded and almost completely destroyed, but the ones located in the large valley – the «Vallone» – adjacent to the Italian front lines were somehow very well protected from enemy fire. The Doberdò plateau was in fact crossed by the main front line and on the very area of exceptionally intense battles that were fought between August 10$^{th}$, 1916, through May 1917, when the Italians reached the village of Iamiano, east of Doberdò. In the wide valley, often mentioned by Settimio Damiani, there were endless

Settimio Damiani and other Italian troopers on the Carso Plateau (1917). The protagonist of our story is the one right in front of the military tent in the background.

Italian depots, huts and barracks, and even small, military cemeteries. Something can still be seen today, especially in the outskirts of the small villages of Bonetti and Ferletti. On the hill in front of the little chapel at Palchisce, many trenches have been restored for historical purposes, as well as many gun emplacements on the hills around Brestovi. In the days preceding the next Italian major offensive, these very sectors were densely populated by Italian soldiers of many different arms and Regiments. At that time, the whole scenery surely appeared «painted» with the gray–green shades of the Italian suits. It was also a most spectacular and impressive display of resources, with every single inch of terrain occupied by men, guns, shells and ammo depots, and vast array of military equipment. A frightening landscape as well, especially for the worn–out Austrian troops on the other side of the valley.

At 18:00 on July 15[th] the Italian artillery fire began once again, this time targeted mainly on the Fornaza sector, where the 61[st] Italian division was deployed, and further north. On the lines occupied by the 54[th] division. The attack of the Italian infantry followed at 20:00 on the same day with Hill 241 being the main goal of the advance. The 61[st] division thus launched its troopers from the Bari, the Siena, and the Sardinia Brigade (again, the «Grenadiers») quickly taking all the enemy lines. In the morning of the 16[th], the Bari and Siena Brigades, in spite of their indomitable courage and fighting spirit, were counter–attacked and pushed back, while the Grenadiers defended their newly acquired positions. At night, nonetheless, Hill 241 was still in enemy hands.

«The fever came back. We were loaded on trucks like animals and immediately taken to Redipuglia where we set up a camp for the night. We could hear a terrible bombardment over the Carso plateau. We saw green flares in the sky all night long – in few hours we will be back in the carnage! On July 14[th] we received the marching orders at night. We marched along roads packed with traffic and every ten paces or so we had to stop, hearing the guns and staring at numberless wounded passing by. This time nobody comes back alive. When we reached the Doberdò valley, very sad and worried, we were deployed in nicely and strongly built trenches. Me and my company were ordered to the line of resistance [second line, right behind the front lines]. On the second night here, we moved to the advanced line. The enemy attacked my sector and we heard a big noise. Then the whistles blowing.... and the order to wear the gas masks, the enemy was launching asphyxiating gas. Shooting furiously we manage to repel the enemy attack, which tried to dislodge us from our advanced positions. Bombs of all kinds were raining over my head.

A captain major of my platoon took a direct hit in the chest and became a corpse immediately [it's captain Antonio Perillo, killed on Hill 241]. I fired 16 magazines without taking my mask off and burned out 4 rifles. After an hour it all becomes calm. My company had suffered many casualties. On July 18<sup>th</sup> the battalion was relieved and we went back to the third line. As soon as we arrived all we heard was about a further advance. A colonel from HQ, talked to us: «Tomorrow we must take the whole Hill 241. At six o'clock the action had begun. Our artillery launched the fire of hell while the enemy counter-attacked with an even denser deluge. The 2<sup>nd</sup> battalion advanced. We are on reserve, but the enemy guns are all over us and the trenches are all upside down. Every now and then we can hear the wounded screaming. We saw four ugly-looking Austrian soldiers passing by, guarded by the Carabinieri, [Italian military police] and we laughed at them. My battalion is ordered to attack, and all the soldiers complain. Today they kill us all. We curse the colonel and the battle gets tougher and tougher. All of a sudden some shrapnel hits a soldier in my team, killing him instantly. It's sheer terror and there are many dead around. My lieutenant, in charge of the company, is badly hit in an arm and is out of the fight. The sergeant takes command of the company, I take command of my platoon. Twenty-two soldiers are left As soon as we reach the.... we are all very pale and exhausted. We are the Regimental command post. We have to resupply the advancing battalions. As soon as we hear this, nobody wants to go. Many times my name is repeated. I come out from a cavern and said, «Yes Sir, what are your orders? »

«Take 20 men and bring immediately some ammo to the 2<sup>nd</sup> platoon!»

I wander across the trenches, but I could find only 5 men.

A small memorial tablet to the fallen Italian soldiers near the hamlet of Bonetti on the Doberdò Plateau. It has been built on the right side of the «S.S. 55» road to Gorizia, Italy.

This photograph, taken from the Visitors Centre in Gradina, east of Doberdò, shows an old military installation which was used by the Italian Army, as training facility, right after the Great War.

Nobody wants to come along. The Regimental command post takes a direct grenade hit. Many are dead or wounded. I go the depot and distribute two crates of bombs to my few men, and then took them along for a while and eventually left them. The officers are not concerned about them. I do not want to be concerned either. Luckily, I was able to find some men to transport the ammos. While projectiles of all kind whistle around us, a runner arrived from the line and told the command, «A platoon of the 5$^{th}$ company is stuck under enemy wire entanglements; they cannot advance nor retreat and the Austrians on their back are killing them all!

On July 19$^{th}$, in the morning, the brigadier colonel paid us a surprise visit and discovered colonel Monti in a cavern [colonel Alberto Monti]. The general, seeing the defeated Regiment, becomes very angry. He told the colonel, «Very good colonel, you are cozily sheltered here, while you do not even know the whereabouts of your Regiment!»

The colonel was replaced and taken to the rear lines immediately. A colonel who has been awarded medals...in a cavern, when the news was spread, the soldiers cheered and were happy about it.

On July 20$^{th}$, the major from the 2$^{nd}$ battalion took command and in the night he ordered the 139$^{th}$ Regiment to relieve us. On July 21$^{st}$ we arrived at the barracks in Palazzo, away from the enemy guns' range. At night, we were bombarded by enemy planes and many soldiers went to sleep outside. Every night we had casualties. After ten days of rest, we headed back to the front line. On August 1$^{st}$ we reached the trenches at Komarie and we were ordered to rebuild and repair them – a work done at night without a single day of rest. After ten days, the whole Siena Brigade went back to S. Pietro d'Isonzo for R&R.»

# The eleventh battle of the Isonzo

On August 17th, 1917, the Italians launched their last major offensive in the Isonzo sector. It was the biggest battle ever fought during the war between Italy and Austria–Hungary. General Cadorna launched 52 divisions, supported by 5,200 guns, against a large number of enemy strongholds, along the middle and the lower Isonzo. Nonetheless, this impressive attack force was halted near Mount San Gabriele.

At the end of July, the International allies of Italy had specifically asked Cadorna to keep the enemy very busy on his front, thus avoiding a major concentration of troops against the nearly–collapsing Russian Army. Thus, the Italian C–in–C devised a comprehensive strategy which encompassed a vast series of attacks from the bridge–head of Tolmino to the Adriatic Sea. Many were the successful breakthroughs of the Italian infantry which managed to cross the Isonzo river in many different sectors. Certainly, the biggest result achieved was the occupation of the entire Bainsizza plateau. The Italians were eventually able to push their lines inside the enemy lines, creating a salient and isolating two of the strongest Austro–Hungarian positions – Mount San Gabriele and Mount Hermada.

After a most violent fight, the Italian 2nd Army, lead by general Luigi Capello, pushed the Austrians back, taking the Bainsizza and Mount Santo. Other enemy strongholds were taken as well by the Duke of Aosta's 3rd Army. In particular, at dawn on August 19th, four corps of the 3rd Army attacked from the Vippacco River to the Adriatic Sea, on the Carso plateau and, along with the VIIIrd corp engaged around the city of Gorizia, achieved many outstanding results. The XXIIIrd corp, lead by the future Italian C–in–C, General Armando Diaz, penetrated the Doberdò sector, heading for Selo (Opatje Selo, now in Slovenia) while trying to reach the strongholds at Brestovica and Lovka. From there, the very same corp should have supported the frontal attack launched against Mount Hermada by the XXIIIrd corp.

The remains of an Italian trench on Mount Brestovi, north of the village of Doberdò. This particular trench system can be reached from Devetachi, on the «S.S. 55» road, following a path heading north.

In spite of all these successes, Cadorna was soon ordered to keep on advancing only if success and sensible strategic gains could be guaranteed. The Italian generalissimo was actually trying to avoid another useless massacre after two full years of terrifying manslaughter and minimum results. Mount Hermada, in particular, had already taken too many times its toll of young blood. The troopers of the Duke of Aosta were going to attack this impressive stronghold and its numberless machine–gun nests once again. Not to mention that, in order to approach this very area, the infantrymen were forced to cross a portion of No-Man's-Land so close to the enemy lines that Italian barbed wire was actually entangled with the enemy's, thus creating impenetrable obstacles all the way up to Mount Hermada.

Nonetheless, the men of the Duke of Aosta proved once again their indomitable courage with sheer determination almost impossible to believe. In fact, it looked absolutely extraordinary that those very same men could attack, once again, on a devastated landscape, scattered with the rotting corpses of friends and comrades, without losing their mind.

«On August 18th, Italy launches another offensive from Mount Nero to the sea. At night, we see the Carso completely ablaze, while flares light up the entire front at night. On the 20th, we see some Austrian platoons of prisoners. Rumors speak of us being once again drafted for manslaughter. In fact, at dawn on August 23rd, we left for the frontline. As soon as we reached the valley we were given plenty of ammo and we proceeded to the line of resistance. Every four paces we had to stop to avoid the searchlights, while shrapnel hit everywhere, all the time and everybody hoped for a bullet…

The 1st battalion is on my left, tasked with resupplying services. We see entire companies of Austrian prisoners, taken by the Grenadiers and the 139th and 140th Regiments, but these very units come back today with heavy casualties. Me and my squad transport food containers, water and bread every night. The enemy airplanes come like birds. Today, for the third day in a row, the Siena Brigade attacks, the bombardment is like the universal deluge. The enemy positions are impossible to take and everybody has to go back to the starting line after the attack. My good luck sees me tasked with supplies and not commanded to fight. Unfortunately, I am exposed to lethal danger anyway. Death falls all around me many times. Every now and then somebody disappears. The enemy is bombarding also the front lines with heavy caliber grenades. The mortar shells especially make a terrible and most frightening noise. The trenches are all destroyed, and corpses are actually buried inside them; it's a real terrifying experience like nobody has never experienced before.

On August 27$^{th}$, we have been grouped with two platoons of engineers in charge of transportation of materials... Every night, when we walk down the road to Selo, taking barbed wire up to the advanced lines, we see many wounded soldiers and dead horses. The enemy bombards us with shrapnel grenades, forcing us to stop quite often, even for fifteen minutes, in order to avoid the deluge. It's terrible to walk down that road. Now we received a new order – horses and trucks have to take supplies to the second line. The Austrians know about our movement on that road and every night it's a storm of fire; dead horses are all around and the stench is terrible. Everything is destroyed, not a single pillar stands. There is plenty of dead of all kinds. On September 4$^{th}$, at dawn, the enemy guns started firing most ferociously, reaching as far as the sea. Our guns reply with a similar fire of hell; flares and searchlights illuminate every sector. The Austrians attack; few of them manage to go back. Today we can see our airplanes engaged in the battle above us and the Austrian guns fire 100 shells per minute at them. Deafening noise comes from the exploding grenades and we can even hear the guns blazing in the distance. From the sea, the hills of the Carso are all fire and smoke. This battle, going on for two days, is the most awesome of all. Oh sweet Jesus, please help and support us fighters and most of all help those poor wounded who are screaming under the rocks.»

The following deployment of Austrian reserves balanced the fight. The scarce Italian advance was nullified when the Austrians took back every single inch of lost ground with violent counter-attacks. On August 29$^{th}$, general Cadorna ordered to halt the offensive, but the 3$^{rd}$ Italian Army kept on engaging the enemy, while general Capello successfully took the Bainsizza plateau. In Selo we find the 31$^{st}$ Regiment of Settimio Damiani, engaged in the above mentioned continuous assaults of the 3$^{rd}$ Italian Army.

Settimio Damiani (left) with other three Italian infantrymen. All these soldiers wear the standard-issue, green-grey military cape. The same wool cloth was used to produce other military outer garments for most cooler climates, such as coats, waistcoats, trousers, and breeches.

This Regiment will then go back to Bertiolo and re-group with the reserves for the Italian High Command until the days of Caporetto.

Following the last «push» of general Cadorna, the Austro–Hungarians were on the verge of total defeat and everybody realized that a further offensive would have completely destroyed them. Settimio Damiani, as well as all his comrades on the Isonzo River, was in similar, desperate conditions. Thanks to his poignant accounts it appears very clear that, all the recent Italian offensives had wasted an incredible amount of blood, energy and resources, without leading to any particular success. Between the major attacks, minor skirmishes never ceased, and the 31$^{st}$ Regiment kept on being launched in battle in the Doberdò sector. Our brave infantryman is often spared the actual fight but is tasked with even more dangerous chores in the support trenches. In fact, while the Siena Brigade runs against the enemy positions, the Austrians heavily shell the Italian rear lines to cut all their vital resupply arteries. From August 18, through the first days of September, the Austrians suffered some 10,000 dead, 45,000 wounded, 30,000 M.I.A. and more that 150 guns lost to the enemy or destroyed. The Italians recorded 40,000 dead, 108,000 wounded, and 18,000 M.I.A.

The result of Cadorna's last «push», forced his enemy to seek help from his German ally to massively counter-attack in the following October, 1917, to avoid total defeat by further Italian offensives. Most oddly, the conquest of the Bainsizza plateau cost Cadorna the forthcoming rout of Caporetto.

«After 24 hours, the infantry ceased fire, but the artillery kept on vomiting fire. The Austrians tried so many times to re-take our positions. After three days of a hurricane of fire, they could not regain a single palm of terrain. On September 7$^{th}$ we were relieved by the Grenadiers. The Siena Brigade goes back, with many casualties, to R&R at San Pietro d'Isonzo.

Me and other ten soldiers have been transferred to the engineers' barracks and we are tasked with feeding the soldiers in the front lines at night. For ten nights I lead a team of 19 soldiers up to Hill 219 through storms of grenades. On the hill there is an Austrian gallery which now hosts up to a battalion of infantrymen, plus 4 apartments for officers and other men. Inside the gallery you cannot even hear the guns. The Austrians built these galleries well before the war. Yesterday we found ten Austrian corpses inside the gallery and also some of ours, not yet buried, as well as many others outside. The smells are terrible and are of all kinds. It's a terrifying sight.

On September 25$^{th}$, the 61$^{st}$ division ordered us to build roads to Selo at night. Every evening before leaving we get feverish. The road to Selo is a storm of grenade, shrapnel, and bullets of all calibers. On October 2$^{nd}$ the 61$^{st}$ division's HQ sentenced to death three engineers found guilty of desertion.

I was there and, in the distance, I saw them shot to death by the firing squad. Many comrades got even closer, but I was not brave enough to do the same. On October 5$^{th}$, two more soldiers were sentenced to death, one from my Regiment, and the other from the 32$^{nd}$. The division commander ordered every company to select its representatives for attending the military trial. Some ten companies were thus represented during the proceedings, while the enemy guns kept on roaring very close. In ten minutes, the judge read the sentence: «in the name of God and by will of the Nation, these soldiers are sentenced to death and will be shot in the back for repeated desertion in front of the enemy.» Those poor devils, heavily guarded by the Carabinieri, started crying, offering to go back and stay in the front lines for the rest of the war, rather than being shot. Nobody listened to their desperate pledges and I heard them screaming. Then, the judge gave us a harsh reprimand, saying, «These tragic events are heart-breaking ones. Do you see how many dead soldiers and war cemeteries are all around us? Each one of us must fight and fulfill his duties, heroically and for our country! These things should never happen again!

Two teams were ordered to form the firing squad. I chose two soldiers from my squad and they left for a nearby hill. I went back to my hut, since I did not want to see the execution, but my commanding officer called me back. The two soldiers confessed their sins to the military chaplains from the 31$^{st}$ and the 32$^{nd}$ Regiments, wrote a last

Italian troopers carrying supplies up to the front lines in the Iamiano Valley - the «vallone» often mentioned by Settimio Damiani. This picture was taken in the summer of 1917, when Luigi Cadorna, the Generalissimo of the Italian Army, was launching his last two major offensives against the Austro-Hungarians, before the Battle of Caporetto.

An Italian infantryman drafting a letter or a diary entry on his trustworthy notepad. The picture was taken in the trenches on the Carso Plateau.

postcard to their families, kissed the priests and each other good-bye. A lieutenant blindfolded them and they had to sit inside a trench. A captain ordered to fire. They were killed instantly. Me and my comrades, deeply moved, got back to our huts and took our lunch without speaking a word. The 31st Regiment got back to the very same sector after 15 days of rest in S. Pietro d'Isonzo.»

While 650 deserters were reported in 1915, more than 5,500 were found guilty of the same offences in the summer of 1917. General Cadorna, ignoring the increasing weariness of his troops and obsessed by the alleged threat of anti-war propaganda, wrote in a letter to his daughter Carla, on June 7th, 1917, «The Austrian war-bulletin speaks of three complete, Italian Regiments which surrendered without firing a single shot. It's the most disgraceful event of the entire war. I will ask the king to disband our three Sicilian Regiments. Sicilians are good soldiers, but they are very weak in front of anti-militaristic propaganda.»

Cadorna was considered a butcher by every Italian soldier, mainly because of his incredibly strict enforcement of military discipline throughout the war. Nonetheless, he was not the only one to treat his men just like puppets, since death sentences for lack of discipline and desertion were tragically frequent on all the other fronts of the Great War. To make things worse, even a simple suspect of desertion often led to a quick trial and immediate execution. Anybody found «guilty» of even temporarily moving away from the front line was considered a deserter and therefore shot. Until the days of Caporetto, this tragic situation kept on escalating to further inhuman violence.

«On October 11 and 12, the enemy launched a terrifying offensive. The attack was soon repelled, with minimum casualties, while all our guns, flares, and searchlights kept on targeting the whole front. I spent a total 53 days in the rear line, tasked with re-supplies, and it was much worse than being in the front line. My underwear was thick with lice. On October 14th, the Regiment had its first lunch at Redipuglia, and then some trucks took us away from this god-forsaken Carsic battlefield. We won't be back anymore. On the 15th we arrived in Codroipo. After many months of battle on the bloody Carso, we hope to enjoy a long rest.»

# The Caporetto rout

At the end of October, 1917, another major Austro–Hungarian offensive, supported by some German crack-battalions, managed to break the Italian frontline after the «Punitive Expedition» of the previous year. This time, quite unexpectedly, the initial success was further exploited with a major invasion of North–East Italy; this caused a devastating rout.

Following the last unsuccessful «push» on the Isonzo, general Luigi Cadorna decided to entrench his men on defensive positions until the Spring of 1918. In spite of these orders, the commander of the Italian 2$^{nd}$ Army, general Luigi Capello – the one who had just conquered the Bainsizza plateau – sought further glory and kept all his men and artillery on the most advanced positions, hoping to boastfully counter–attack any possible enemy advance. A major misunderstanding, between these two commanders, was later addressed as the principal cause for the dangerous inconsistencies in the Italian defenses which were exploited by the enemy attack. The truth is Cadorna never knew Capello's real plans and simply assumed that all his subordinates would have retreated to much stronger, defensive positions. To make things worse, the Italian HQ never listened to detailed and reliable information about the forthcoming enemy offensive, even when some deserters presented the official attack plans to the Italian Intelligence.

As we just mentioned, all the guns of the 2$^{nd}$ Army and most of its men were being kept in too advanced positions, while the rear lines were poorly manned and reserves were too far away. Settimio Damiani and his «Siena» Brigade, for instance, were part of the Italian HQ reserve Regiments, deployed between Pozzecco and Virco Villa, on the outskirts of the village of Bertiolo, the furthest sector from where the breach would have taken place.

At 2:00 o'clock on October 24th 1917, the Austrian guns launched a terrifying deluge of shells and lethal gas on the whole upper and middle Isonzo front. Six hours later their infantry Regiments attacked, and by the end of the day the line had been successfully breached in many sectors. Three days later, German troops occupied Cividale del Friuli, and the following day they captured Udine. In the first days of November all the bridges on the Piave River were destroyed by the Italians, as their last resort to temporarily stop the enemy advance, reorganize, and desperately try to counter-attack. All the most expensive, but minimal, gains of the previous eleven Italian offensives were erased in few hours, while the whole regions of Friuli, Cadore, and Carnia were invaded by the enemy.

«On the 24th, we received new backpacks. We cleaned ourselves up and used some straw to take a good sleep. On the very same day we received some parcels from the charity and support committees of Bologna. On the night of the 24th, while fast asleep, the lieutenant in charge of our company woke us up, ordering to prepare ourselves to leave for the new front immediately. The platoon commander made sure to wake up everybody. We were quite happy because even after only twelve days of rest, we were leaving for a new front and not for that darn Carso. At 4 o'clock on October 25th, we gathered in the courtyard, all geared up for battle. Food was distributed. Then we started marching. At 14:00 pm we make our first stop in a valley close to Udine. Sentries were deployed all around us. Nobody could leave, even if temporarily to get food and water. Luckily we were distributed wine and sardines and then some other food. At 15:00 we started marching again, and I received from the Regiment's postman a postal-order from America with 72 liras, but I did not have time to cash it. It got dark and we did not know our destination. We passed Udine and we saw many soldiers. We asked for information, but nobody knew anything. My feet were very tired and… I did not feel like keeping on marching; many soldiers dragged behind and fell to the ground like mules. Eventually at 23:00 we stopped and we simply fell to the ground, scattered like sheep. The lieutenant ordered to set up a camp with tents. I did not have enough strength left, so I simply slept on the grass, dead tired. During my entire military life I had never marched for such a long time. Dawn arrived, but I could not close my eyes. We were given coffee but not bread. Then we received half a bread loaf each; we were starving. Eventually we heard from Alpine troops and Bersaglieri that the enemy was quickly advancing, passing through Caporetto and Cividale, and capturing much of our supplies. Ever since October $22^{nd}$ they have been fiercely attacking, and only thanks to a miracle we could cope with this event. In the afternoon of October $26^{th}$ I quickly ate some pasta. The battalion commander arrived and ordered, «Come on, stand up and let's leave immediately!»

All the scared platoon commanders had to gather their men together like sheep.

The first unmistakable symptoms of defeat appear also in front of Settimio Damiani's eyes. The leaders are frightened and lost, while their men do not know what to do. Run away or refuse to fight are certainly the most common feelings amongst troopers left without real command and precise directions, while morale had never been so low. Later, in the last days of November 1917, the Austrian general Boroevič elaborated on this situation by declaring that the Italian soldiers had deeply felt the increasing lack of command from their leaders.

Settimio Damiani marched for almost 40 miles, leaving Bertiolo and heading for the sector of Mount Jauer – Mount Cavallo, which was going to be violently hit by the Austro–German vanguards of the invading Krauss and Stein battle-groups. The «Siena» Brigade, so hastily deployed in combat, was therefore integrated into the Italian $2^{nd}$ Army.

«At 16:00 PM my battalion started marching very slowly due to the heavy traffic all over the village. Trucks, guns, and many civilians with their families and children were literally fleeing the sector. The road was always packed; the movement was extraordinary. After marching all night long I was dead tired. At dawn, on October $27^{th}$, I arrived in a hamlet close to Mount Cavallo. I could hear the guns. We ate our meal and then we were distributed hand grenades. I barely had the time to send a soldier from my company to fetch a bottle of wine and some ham for me. I did not have the time to get my 3 Liras

Italian troopers rest briefly on their way to the breached frontlines around Caporetto (October 1917). Settimio Damiani marched for almost 40 miles, heading for the very sector which was going to be violently hit by Austro-German vanguards. The «Siena» Brigade, hastily deployed in combat, was therefore going to fight a most ill-fated battle.

change; «boom!» the guns were roaring and the 1st battalion was immediately deployed on the front line. A young lieutenant of the class of 1899 was at my side. I was shaking like a leaf on a tree. The Germans were rapidly advancing. There is a little church at some 10 yards from us.»

The Germans were particularly feared by the Italian soldiers. In spite of many fraternization episodes with the Austrian troops, which eventually lead to mutual respect and acknowledgment of similar fighting strength, the German warriors were always considered some sort of super-human fighters and therefore a major threat.

As we've just seen, most of the Italian guns, dangerously left on advanced positions – after the conquest of the Bainsizza plateau – were quickly captured or destroyed by the enemy.

Therefore, Settimio Damiani, as well as all the other Italian soldiers, could not be supported by any artillery barrage and was thus left «naked» in front of the enemy. Due to this major strategic mistake and many other tactical errors and mishaps, the Italian infantrymen soon would have been surrounded and taken prisoner.

On October 27[th], in the evening, the 3[rd] Schützen Regiment (from the 22[nd] Schützen division of the Krauss battle–group) attacked the Mount Jauer – Mount Cavallo sector, near Mount Le Zuffine. This Regiment was successfully supported by some units of the 50[th] Austro–Hungarian division from the Stein battle–group. During this attack, the Italian troops deployed on Mount Carnizza, Bocchetta di S. Antonio, and at the foot of Mount Joanaz (namely, the 272[nd] e 273[rd] Regiments of the «Potenza» Brigade, one Regiment of Bersaglieri and the «Siena» Brigade), were forced to hastily retreat to a new line, west of the above mentioned Bocchetta di S. Antonio, while few defenders left in the original positions fought to the last man, thereby delaying the enemy advance. Settimio Damiani was amongst the retreating troopers and would be surrounded and captured. General Cadorna himself, in an official bulletin earlier that day, had foreseen such an unfortunate event. He was certainly well aware of the risk of encirclement of his troops that were hastily sent to stop the invasion. In particular, the bulletin advised that «Following a further progress of the invasion on the left of our 2[nd] Army, our troops, currently deployed on Mount Maggiore and Mount Cavallo, currently risk being fully encircled.»

For the Italians, the Caporetto rout meant 12,000 K.I.A., 30,000 wounded and 265,000 P.O.W.s. Furthermore, total destruction and gruesome violence – as vividly reported in Farewell to arms by Ernest Hemingway – were brought to all the invaded territories of North–Eastern Italy, up to the very Piave River, where the Italian retreat eventually stopped. The enemy now was not only allegedly invading Italy - it had done it for real.

«All of a sudden, the enemy start bombarding us. The small outpost is completely destroyed, with many casualties and two soldiers instantly killed. At about 10:00 on October 27$^{th}$, the enemy was advancing, protected by machine–guns barrage fire. We counter–attacked as furiously as we could but were left without the support of even a single gun. I fired 64 bullets and two flares. I could see them advancing and many were killed. In the afternoon, the incoming fire became terrible – the Germans were at ten yards from us. On my left and on my right I saw white flags – soldiers were surrendering. I run away, risking to be then punished as deserter, but I did not want to surrender. I run away along the valley, while enemy guns started pounding it as well; many wounded here were screaming for help. When I reached a nearby village, I found many German soldiers. I did not realize I was surrounded and I thought they were our prisoners. A German soldier pointed his rifle at me, ordering to drop mine immediately. As I understood about the encirclement I dropped my gun and the German took me in an alley where other prisoners had already gathered. I was completely shocked and dead tired. I saw some other three thousands prisoners from various units, and I took a bit of heart. Many Germans, passing by, asked me for food, and I gave them almost everything I had in my backpack, since I thought that war was over for me. In the evening I arrived in a village in the Mount Nero sector and they let us stop. The whole 1st battalion of the 31$^{st}$ infantry Regiment has been taken prisoner.»

It goes without saying that the odyssey of Settimio Damiani did not end with his capture. Ever since that tragic October 27$^{th}$, 1917, our protagonist spent the rest of the Great War in many prisoner camps in Austria and Germany. Starved, barely dressed, and sometimes even almost

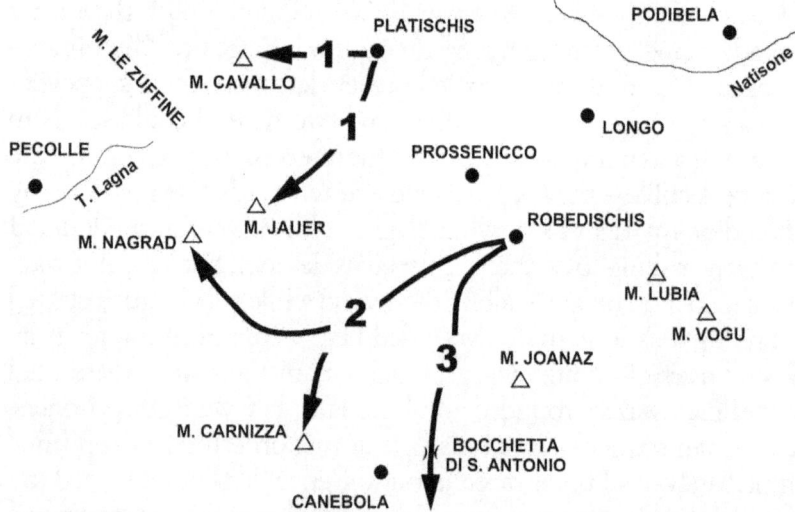

**1** 3° reggimento Schützen della 22a divisione
e II battaglione del 18° reggimento fanteria della 50a divisione austro-ungarica

**2** XV brigata da montagna della 50a divisione
e III battaglione del 7° reggimento della 55a divisione austro-ungarica

**3** altri reparti della 50a divisione austro-ungarica

The close-up map of the battle zone where Settimio Damiani was taken prisoner on November 27, 1917, while trying to stop the Austro-Hungarian advance following the Caporetto rout.

naked in the harsh, northern Europe climate, he skirted a miserable death every single day. Nonetheless, he stoically managed to keep on writing his diary even when, ravenous for food, he had to barter his trustworthy pen for some crackers.

# Imprisonment

During the Great War, imprisonment most certainly meant escaping machine–guns and shell fire but always led to months of misery, starvation and illness, often with lethal consequences. Prisoners died in the camps mostly during the winter months, when the harsh climate became the second worst threat after famine. At night, in many prison camps of Central Europe, during the last months of 1917, the temperature went as low as -86° degrees. Many prisoners, suffering from diarrhoea, were forced to use latrines outside their barracks; in the morning many were found completely frozen and dead. What could have been more terrible than cheating death so many times on a battlefield, only to die miserably in a latrine of a concentration camp?

Most of the Italian P.O.W.s were interned in Austro–Hungaric camps, namely at Mauthausen, Austria, and at Theresienstadt, Bohemia. Also known as «Kriegsgefangenenlager» (camps for prisoners of war), these camps were made of many small huts, completely surrounded by thick barbed wire and blood–thirsty sentries everywhere. As also happened during the Second World War, this basic layout was also used by all the other belligerent countries, when it came to P.O.W. management. The «Kriegsgefangenenlager», also called the city of those about to die, was a place where famine drove people crazy. Many official reports spoke of Italian soldiers scavenging the trash for food remains or even eating grass, soil, and paper. Daily calories per soldier never accounted for more than 900 calories – the «menu» served to the prisoners was in fact almost too absurd to believe: some coffee for breakfast and boiled water with turnip leaves or cabbage at both lunch and dinner. The most nutritious part of the diet was a single potato and a thin slice of wheat bread per day.

Twice a week, an occasional herring and a very small piece of meat (both not too fresh) could be granted. In spite of their starving conditions, many Italians, looking literally like walking bones, were often tasked with tough forced labors as part of the «Arbeiter Kompanien» – the working companies. These groups of prisoners, 200 or 300 per unit, had to cut trees and work in nearby mines. Their food rations were slightly better than the normal ones, but these prisoners were often beaten to death if they did not literally break their backs working all day long.

These camps were created in order to cope with the incredible high number of prisoners who were coming from the massive battles and were made up of thousands and thousands of men; this had taken place ever since the beginning of the Great War. Normal prisons were in fact not enough to handle all the men captured in battle. The prison of Mauthausen created in 1914 was amongst the first, and 30 years later it was tragically used again for similar grim purposes. It was the main camp used for Italian prisoners. Every hut could host up to 250 men on a mere 390 sq. yards. The rain and the cold leaked inside which turned the huts into even muddier, freezing hovels. Needless to say, it was incredibly easy to fall badly sick.

Prisoners slept on the ground with the luckiest ones using a little straw as makeshift mattresses. Clean underwear was not available; a very few men had a blanket. All around them, rifles, machine-guns, and even artillery was ready to fire at point-blank range at anybody trying to escape or even to simply protest these sub-human treatments.

While their soldiers died by the thousands in Austrian lagers, the politicians in Rome were reluctant to send them help. One sixth of the Italian prisoners never came home. The Italian Foreign Minister Sidney Sonnino was strongly against sending any aid to the prisoners mostly because he feared that more and more troopers would have then deserted, hoping to finally escape the horrors of war for a quick and easy stay at the Austrians camps. Furthermore, Sonnino did not want to offer the Austrians such an easy way to steal Italian food and provisions which could have been quickly confiscated upon delivery –in spite of these fears, many Italian prisoners reported in their letters and diaries that their captors were particularly respectful of the very strict but fair rules when it came to personal items, goods, and parcels addressed to each single prisoner. The Italian government kept on refusing help almost until the end of the war, indirectly sentencing many of them to death. To make things worse, even the Italian generals were totally deaf to their men's desperate pleas, considering all the prisoners deserters and therefore not worth even a single morsel of bread.

Luckily, many civilian committees, often privately funded, sent a total 18 million parcels of food to all the Italian prisoners during the Great War. Furthermore, for the first time in history, the Italian Red Cross took part in these humanitarian efforts by organizing massive shipments of bread and facilitating communication between the prisoners and their relatives at home.

The official records report about 100,000 dead Italian prisoners in the Austro–German camps, a figure consistent with one sixth of the 600,000 total casualties of the Great War. Out of 600,000 total casualties during the war, it's an impressively high ratio, especially when compared to other countries' numbers. For example, 18,000 French prisoners died in German camps. Fourteen thousand Austrians suffered the same fate in Italy, out of 480,000 casualties in three years of conflict. We are talking about a mere average 3%, compared to the Italian 17%. It goes without saying that quite oddly, all the Italian troopers had more chances to die in enemy prisons, than on the battlefield. Following these considerations, Settimio Damiani's diary, delivered to his relatives in person, acquires an even more priceless historical value.

«Only our HQ managed to avoid capture. We thought the Germans would feed us, but we received no food at all. I regretted to have given their soldiers my cans of meat and my crackers earlier on. I was very hungry and luckily I still had two crackers and a some canned ham in my backpack. I ate some of my provisions and at night it started raining. I was left only with my shirt and pants, without my coat and my blanket, I was all wet and shivering like a leaf. I was thinking, «I did not die in so many battles and now I am probably going to die as prisoner!»

Around midnight I heard some voices: the prisoners had been granted to sleep inside a church nearby. Inside I could warm myself up a bit, but I was still too wet and did not have anything dry to put on. Then, on the morning of the 28$^{th}$, we were grouped together, while it kept on raining, and we did not receive even a single drop of coffee. By noon, there was no hope to receive a piece of bread either, so I ravenously took a morsel of a cracker I had been saving. We kept on marching; where will these scoundrels take us? Night came and still we did not know where we were going.

Around 23:00 we met another group of prisoners. It was still raining and I was wet as a fish; hunger and thirst were eating me alive. It would have been better to die, rather than suffer like that. We spent three hours on a bridge. Then I saw a light in the distance and I ran to it, out in the country, where I found some other prisoners around a bonfire. I warmed myself up but all of a sudden a group of sentries came on us...

We had to keep on marching. I could not feel my feet anymore. The pain was terrible... I was wearing socks made of sackcloth and my feet were bleeding. After marching for another three kilometers, I fell to the ground, crying, although the Germans wanted me to stand up and keep on walking. I managed to explain that I was exhausted and a soldier was kind enough to send me inside the ruins of a church, where other exhausted prisoners have already been sheltered. I walked around the ruins, found some wood and started a fire, and then I could properly dry off. In the morning we marched again and I saw a battalion of German soldiers carrying Italian materials, supplies, and pack animals.

The prisoners had to travel along a country road, while the main one was reserved for soldiers, thus free to move all their equipment without delay. All of a sudden, a cart gets stuck in the mud. The prisoners simply observed the scene but were hastily ordered to help, when an officer pointed a gun at us. Some twenty of us pushed the cart out of the mud, but our group could barely put together the strength of just a single man.

On June 31st, I arrived at a P.O.W.s camp where some other three thousand prisoners were being kept. Barbed wire was all around us and most of us did not even have the strength to breathe. Our hunger was unbearable. Eventually we heard some rumours about food being distributed. In the afternoon, in fact, we received a can of meat and a bread loaf to be shared amongst each three prisoners. Bread is black and very hard, but we would eat it even if it was a piece of stone. Hunger is still great and sends us walking backwards, instead of keep on marching. I had to walk until night, while my feet were badly hurting. Eventually I fell to the ground and a good German sent me inside a nearby hut, where I slept for the rest of the night. In the morning two sentries sent us away and regrouped us with other marching prisoners. It started raining again. I found a piece of paper and I used it to protect my body; hunger was terrible. I run in the fields to eat roots just like a bird. We did not know where we would make the next stop. Every now and then the sentries shoot at prisoners trying to leave the marching group.

We stopped for a while in a village, thinking that we would have received some food. Instead, our captors left us grouped in the middle of the road and went to eat by themselves. We went looking for the local families, asking for a piece of bread. They were good people, but more starved than us and we left without any bread as well. Along with two other prisoners I found the only family which could give us some apples and roots and a little girl offered me a cigarette. I wanted to repay her with 2 Liras, but she did not accept my money. It seems like I received the whole world, so I started marching again feeling a bit better. When night came I saw many lights in the distance.... there were hundreds of prisoners, so I hoped to receive some food. Since I was at the very end of the line, after waiting for an hour, I did not receive anything – what a sufferance! Then I joined some prisoners to warm myself up a bit, but the rain did not stop and there was no shelter. Taking a big chance I climbed on some roofs to fetch wooden boards and start a fire – the machine guns surrounding us fired short bursts from time to time and many of us were killed while fetching wood in this way.

I know many soldiers of my battalion who have been taken as prisoners. I was left alone with a Sicilian, a guy in much worse conditions than mine. He sold his tunic to a Russian prisoner for 9 oz. of bread. When I saw his bread my eyes went totally crazy. Hunger was devouring me; the cold was hitting my veins hard; the rain kept on falling. Eventually, on October 30$^{th}$ we were grouped together and then moved out to the countryside. We were then split in different groups and sent to sleep in a stable. It felt like sleeping in a hotel. Since I did not have my blanket anymore, I stole an abandoned one, belonging to another soldier – he had his mantel and his coat anyway.

In the evening each one of us received a cup full of crackers and half a cup of marsala wine. I took some heart. Me and another prisoner made a bonfire. We cooked a tin of cabbage and I could finally eat some food. On November 1st we were ordered to leave for Germany. Everybody was happy thinking about better treatment for prisoners in Germany. In the evening we arrived at the railway station in Ljubljana. The cold was getting through our bones and we were hungry like lions. I was very unlucky since I had to travel on an open wagon...

On November 2$^{nd}$ we made a stop in another Austrian station where I received some cabbage soup and 7 oz. of bread. Upon getting back on the train, I chose a closed wagon this time. I was packed inside like a sardine; the Germans sealed the wagon and everybody could not move without hurting somebody else. Everybody kept on cursing. Everybody went crazy without being able to scratch himself because of lice tormenting us. We were treated much worse than animals and people had to urinate and evacuate in the very wagon. On the 5$^{th}$ day of the journey, we arrived in German territory and they took us to a village. Here, inside an industrial building, we took a bath and received a piece of bread and half a cup of tea. Upon going back to the train many prisoners could not find their shoes and had to walk barefooted. Sixty prisoners per wagon, all piled up on each other.

On November 6$^{th}$, in the evening, we finally reach our destination. In the morning we saw many prisoners of different nations, packed inside the huts – French, Russian, English, Belgian prisoners... We sleep on straw mattresses and we have a blanket. Food is scarce and disgusting; also in Germany prisoners are poorly treated. In the morning we get half a cup of something they call coffee, made with grass and without sugar. At lunch some gasoline-smelling soup and 7 oz. of black bread – we devour everything since we are starving. In the evening we hit our mattresses, always incredibly hungry. When they distribute bread in the evening, they force us to queue outside in the cold, for one or two hours. Eventually we receive a 2.2 lbs bread loaf for each group of ten prisoners. Upon sharing it there is always a brawl and he who makes portions is always covered with curses and insults.

In this camp there must be at least a 1000 huts with prisoners from all nations. The Italians suffer the most. At night, we have to put our shoes under our straw mattresses, so as not to get them stolen by scoundrels who would then re-sell them to the French for a piece of bread or a few crackers. In spite of our common Latin blood, the French could bleed us dry if only they could. They have been here for much longer now and they seem to be in charge of supplies; therefore they are doing much better than us and they are not starving. They could easily help some of the Italians in the worst conditions, but they don't. They have... thousands of Italians with gold and clothes. I had only a fountain pen. I bartered it for two crackers. Hunger is not my only misery, also the cold bites me hard. I am left only with pants and a cotton shirt. One day I had the great idea of cutting my blanket in pieces and make a shirt, a cap and some wrappings for my feet. Luckily I also had a pair of worn out socks which I used for stitching cotton thread.

After longing for it for such a long time, on November 8[th] I received my first postcard to inform my parents about being imprisoned in Germany. In the morning, we have just five minutes to wake up and go outside to take half a cup of hot water and try to clean ourselves. We do not have the strength to move our legs. We

always think about food. Italian prisoners always talk about food. People often say, «Oh God, how much rice I threw away while I was in the trenches! If only I had that very stale bread I threw away during the first year of war, I would be rich!»
Many prisoners risk their lives trying to enter the French and the British areas, seeking food. The Germans quickly beat them to death, using their swords. Many have been hospitalized for this reason. When anything goes wrong, and the culprit cannot be found, all the prisoners are forced inside their huts. Many prisoners who smoke use some straw from their mattresses in their pipes. When the Germans discover them, they are punished very harshly.

On December 12$^{th}$, we were moved to another camp and we hoped to be treated a little better. We travelled with a train, in very cold weather which bit our bones. We almost died without any means to warm us up. On the 14$^{th}$ we arrived in a camp where other Russian prisoners were kept. We spent three days here, eating only carrots, turnips and beetroots – I thought I was going to die.

Luckily, on December 16$^{th}$, 200 prisoners were grouped and sent to the station. We had to wait four hours for the train, while the cold was unbearable and it was snowing. We made groups of 30/40 prisoners and stuck together to warm ourselves. On December 17$^{th}$ we arrived at the concrete fortress, near Strasbourg, where we found many other Russian and Romanian prisoners. The food had slightly improved and we are waiting to be assigned to various types of labours.»

Settimio Damiani speaks of the German city of Strasbourg, Germany, while, in fact, he was interned at the Festung Hohensalzburg Castle in Salzburg, Austria. This is mainly due to his obvious lack of comprehensive geographical notions and the similarities between the names of the two cities. The castle in Strasbourg was never used as a prison during the Great War, while many international prisoners were kept in the massive stronghold, built in Salzburg, back in 1077. During its long history it served, in fact, as a refuge for the archbishops, a military barracks, and a prison.

«Once a week they let us take a bath and finally we got clean underwear, a pair of boots, and coat. We took a medical test and I was chosen with other 150 prisoners to work in a factory, replacing Russian prisoners, who are less suitable for this task. I spent the Christmas holidays of 1917 in prison and on Christmas day I ate turnips with a piece of meat as hard as donkey's. In the evening the priest of Strasburg sent a cigar to all the prisoners, since he could not offer any food.

On December 26$^{th}$, I was tasked, along with two other prisoners, with unloading a train wagon full of coal. In this factory where I work, there are three thousand civilians and 150 prisoners. They give us one mark a day and, according to our different skills, we are assigned to work with different groups of civilians. My work is: in the morning I mix soil with a machine; then I take it to the furnace, and, with the help of a civilian, I put it into the kiln. I often cut wood and help transport iron to the furnace. The civilians here care for me; I do a little extra work for them and every morning they bring me food from home: potatoes, occasional pieces of bread, and quite often milk or leftovers. I eat everything when nobody is watching me. I spend all the money I earn here.

On January 20$^{th}$, 1918, we received the long-awaited postcard to write home for Easter. The German sergeant took us to the nearby village to visit the church. Some thirty prisoners took the Holy Communion. Every Sunday an Italian-speaking priest from Strasburg comes to our barracks to say Mass. A German soldier, who recently got back from the Italian front, brought and sold a bottle of olive oil for 30 Marks. The Germans are lacking many kinds of food these days. Soap made with gypsum sells for 5 marks apiece, while wooden clogs cost ten marks. I made myself a pair of socks using some rags.

On April 27$^{th}$, with immense joy, after seven months of prison, I received news from my parents. On May 4$^{th}$ I heard about many parcels delivered in Strasburg for the prisoners. We could not wait to get them. We cheered with each other thinking about them! In the

Standing high over the city of Salzburg, the magnificent «Hohensalzburg» dominates the city, and is nowadays its main tourist attraction. During the Great War it served as a military facility for P.O.W.s where Settimio Damiani spent the last months of his imprisonment.

evening we gathered to see whether there was anything for us. A German soldier read our dog–tag numbers aloud and distributed the goods. I was lucky to get one parcel addressed to me. Many did not receive anything, so they went back to their bunks, crying in despair. The luckiest of us shared some bread with our comrades, but we could not satisfy all of them....»

The diary of Settimio Damiani abruptly ends, on page 76, without any explanation. Most certainly, it was impossible for our infantryman to keep on writing due to the lack of pen and paper – priceless and somehow forbidden commodities in the German prisons. As many other war veterans, when Settimio Damiani returned to Italy and then permanently moved to the U.S., he never spoke too much about his experience. His terrible, but also most fortunate survival marked him for the rest of his life.

He miraculously managed to save his life, while most of his comrades never came home from the Austro–German «Kriegsgefangenenlager», yet his soul bore an eternal, deep scar forever.

Nowadays Settimio Damiani can be considered a real patriot; he was a simple, decent man, completely alien to any rhetorical propaganda and vainglorious ideal. He simply fought for his life, while always fulfilling numberless, highly demanding and dangerous tasks. A unique sense of duty and a superhuman endurance of incredible miseries made him a true, ordinary hero of all times. We can also add that Settimio Damiani was a no–nonsense hard worker who faced every single challenge in his life, no matter how hard and challenging, with undisputed and indomitable willpower and sheer dedication. Even though Settimio Damiani permanently moved back to the U.S. after the war, his intense patriotic experience can surely consecrate him as the icon of an Italian forever, unmistakably embedded in that very portion of Italy's long history.

Flags and banners should be raised for Settimio Damiani, as well as to honor the millions of young lives prematurely snuffed out during the Great War.

Today, tomorrow, and forever may the spirit of remembrance be kept alive, along with pride, joy, love, and the most sincere appreciation of all those men who gave everything they had for a better world.

The Homewood Memorial cemetery near Chicago Heights, IL USA. Here rest Settimio Damiani and his brother Cesare.

The tomb of Settimio Damiani in the Homewood Memorial cemetery near Chicago Heights, IL USA. The Italian infantryman died in the US at the age of 89, in 1979.

Today, the relatives of Settimio Damiani remember him as a most quiet and discreet person who spoke of the war only on rare occasions. One of the last memories, forever embedded in the heart of his nephew Tim, pictures Settimio as a sweet and gentle grandfather who often ate up to the very skin of his potatoes, whispering, «I really know what starving means!.»

# Appendix 1
# The medals awarded to Settimio Damiani

The official military record – «Foglio Matricolare» – of each Italian soldier includes much information, such as the detailed service, the medals awarded, etc. Such document lives a life of its own, even after a soldier has been discharged and has permanently left the army. Settimio Damiani's makes no exception, and well after his return to the US included further medals awarded to our brave Italian trooper.

In particular, where his military record says «Campagne e Azione di merito» (Campaigns and Meritorious Actions) the authors of this book discovered that Settimio Damiani was awarded three different medals. The first two medals were awarded to all the Italian veterans of the Great War, with the current, official motivation, «For having served in the war of 1915-1918 and the campaigns of 1916-1917, as per the Italian Royal Order in Council number 1241, dated July 29th, 1920..» These two medals were minted with the bronze of the enemy guns captured on the battlefields and were paid for by the Italian government.

In 1922, following the Italian Royal Order in Council number 1299, dated January 19th, 1922) a third medal was awarded to all the Italian veterans of the Great War, but this time each soldier would have to pay for it. Designed by Italian artist Mario Nelli, quite oddly this medal was never granted to Settimio Damiani – in fact, his military record does not show the official authorization to buy and use this particular award.

The actual third medal awarded to Settimio Damiani was created as per the Italian Royal Order in Council number 1362, dated October 19th, 1922. This medal simply celebrated Italy's unity, officialized during its recent, major war effort. An outstanding incongruousness appears: this very medal was awarded exclusively to all the mothers and the widows of Italian soldiers who fought and died during the Great War, and not to the actual soldiers. It's hard to blame this inconsistency on mere carelessness:

the military records – especially the information about medals and awards – were always thoroughly double-checked and officialized by more than one officer.

Thus, after further research, the authors of this book found out about a second, official motivation for this very medal. It appeared that this award was also granted to the relatives of any Italian soldier who served and died in any war fought between 1848 and 1918. Cesare Damiani, one of Settimio's brothers, returned to Italy few years before the Great War and died in 1913. Italy had recently fought a previous war against Libya in 1911-1912. If Cesare had fought in this conflict and died of wounds right after its end, we could possibly explain why Settimio was eventually authorized to use this medal as Cesare's next of kin.

Most unfortunately, Settimio Damiani never knew about this medal, as he permanently moved back to the US two years before it was granted. None of his relatives in Italy ever claimed or bought it.

# Appendix 1 - The medals awarded to Settimio Damiani

The original military record - «Foglio Matricolare» - of private Settimio Damiani (courtesy of the Italian Ministry of Defence). The original document is part of the military archives of Ascoli Piceno. This type of document lives a life of its own, even after a soldier has been discharged and has permanently left the army. Settimio Damiani's makes no exception, and well after his return to the US recorded further medals awarded to our brave Italian trooper.

The first of the two medals awarded to all the Italian veterans of the Great War, with the current, official motivation, «For having served in the war of 1915-1918 and the campaigns of 1916-1917» as per the Italian Royal Order in Council number 1241, dated July 29, 1920. This medal was minted with the bronze of the enemy guns captured on the battlefields and were paid for by the Italian government.

Appendix 1 - The medals awarded to Settimio Damiani 135

The first of the two medals awarded to all the Italian veterans of the Great War, with the current, official motivation, «For having served in the war of 1915-1918 and the campaigns of 1916-1917» as per the Italian Royal Order in Council number 1918, dated December 16, 1920. Also this medal was minted with the bronze of the enemy guns captured on the battlefields and were paid for by the Italian government.

The third medal awarded to Settimio Damiani, created as per the Italian Royal Order in Council number 1362, dated October 19, 1922. This medal celebrated Italy's unity, achieved and acknowledged during the Great War. This medal had to be paid for by any Italian soldier or a relative authorized to claim it.

# Glossary

Attrition: Strategy of wearing down the enemy through continual attack and pressure

Battalion: a military unit composed of a headquarters and two or more companies, batteries, or similar units

C-in-C: Commander in chief

Carabinieri: Military Police

Central Powers: The Central Powers was the term used to describe the wartime alliance of Germany and Austria-Hungary against the Entente Powers. Later the term was extended to include Turkey and Bulgaria

Commanding Officer or C.O. : the officer in command of an infantry battalion or cavalry regiment.

Creeping barrage: Artillery fire from each unit advancing in stages of one line at a time

Brigade: a tactical and administrative unit composed of a headquarters, one or more units of infantry or armour, and supporting units

Deluge: an overwhelming amount or number

Dog Tag: an identification tag (as for military personnel or pets)

Duckboards: A board which was laid down on trench floors and flooded fields to help stop soldiers from sinking into the muddy ground

Dug-Outs: Name given to the rough living space made in a trench

Entente Powers: The Entente powers, or Allied powers, during World War I were Great Britain, France, and Russia. The United States joined the war to assist the Entente powers against the Central powers.

Entrenched: To be fixed or deeply rooted in an area

Gallipoli: Scene of an unsuccessful naval expedition in 1915, off the Dardanelles.

Gas: various poisonous gases used during the Great War

HQ: Headquarters

Latrines: Toilets

Marsala: a fortified Sicilian wine that varies from dry to sweet and is often used in cooking

Missing in action or M.I.A.: a member of the armed forces whose whereabouts following a combat mission are unknown and whose death cannot be established beyond reasonable doubt

No-man's-land: The dangerous land between two opposing trench lines

Non-commissioned officer or N.C.O.: a subordinate officer (as a sergeant) in the army, air force, or Marine Corps appointed from among enlisted personnel

Over-the-top: the act of climbing out of a trench and going forward into battle

Parados: the rear edge of a trench (the opposite of a parapet)

Parapet: built up front edge of a trench, which protected men

Plateau: a usually extensive land area having a relatively level surface raised sharply above adjacent land on at least one side

Prisoner of war or P.O.W.: a combatant who is imprisoned by an enemy power during or immediately after an armed conflict.

Propaganda: Information given to show something or someone in a biased way

R&R: acronym for Rest and Recuperation or Rest and Recreation

Ration (or rationing): A limited portion or allowance of food or goods

Reconnaissance or Recon: Investigation or exploration or something

Regiment: a military unit consisting usually of a number of battalions

Rout: an overwhelming, disorderly defeat

Salient: Prominent or projecting part of the line often protruding out from the main front line

Shell shock: Medical condition caused by prolonged exposure to the distressing experiences of trench warfare

Shrapnel: a projectile that consists of a case provided with a powder charge and a large number of usually lead balls and that is exploded in flight

Start line: the line from where an attack commences

Trench fever: An influenza-like disease spread by lice

Trench Foot: A rotting disease of the feet caused by overexposure to the cold and damp of the trenches

Trench warfare: Form of fighting whereby two sides fight each other from opposing trenches

Triple Alliance: Name of the defensive alliance between Germany, Austro-Hungary and Italy

Very Lights: a variety of coloured signal flares, fired from a special pistol (Very pistol) created by E. W. Very (1847–1907), U.S. inventor

Wire: barbed wire

# Bibliography

-Tenente Orlando, (1929) Manuale scuola allievi ufficiali, Lucca, Artiglieria da campagna, Stabilimento Grafico A.S.

- Amministrazione Comunale di Posina, (2000) Il diario della guerra in Val Posina

- Ercoli, E, Le medaglie al valore, al merito e commemorative, Milano, Ediz. I.D.L.

- Amm. Comunale e Pro Arsiero, (1966) Arsiero e il settore Astico Posina, Fuga Edizioni

- De Mori, G, (1930) Chiostro Ossario dei Caduti di Guerra alla SS. Trinità di Schio, Schio, Ediz. Marzari

- De Mori, G, (1931) Vicenza nella Grande Guerra, Vicenza, Tipografia Rumor

- Corni-Bucciol-Schwarz, (1990) Inediti della Grande Guerra, Trieste, Edizioni Fachin

- Girotto, L. (1995) La lunga Trincea 1915-1918, Rossato.

- Morittu, G. (1996) Guerre e decorazioni 1948 – 1945, Padova

- Castagna, Gattera, Compero, (2005) Il Battaglione alpini Monte Berico. G. Rossato

- Associazione Pro Malo,(1998) Malo nella Grande Guerra, Vicenza, Ediz. Ist. San Gaetano

- Tenenete Ferrari U. S., (1923) Ricordi di guerra , Schio, Topografia Pasubio Editrice

- Mantoan, N. (1988) Bombe a mano italiane 1915-18, R.C. Graf.

- Ass. Naz. del Fante, (1996) Storia della Fanteria italiana, Treviso, Tipolitografia FG

- Rauch, C. (1994) Storia dell'I. R. Rgt degli Schützen dell'alta Austria, Trento, Effe & Erre

- Ministero della Guerra (1925) Brigate di Fanteria, Roma, Libreria dello Stato

- Ministero della Guerra (1925) Brigate di Fanteria, Siena, Libreria dello Stato

- M. Eichta (2000), Braunau – Katzenau – Mitterndorf 1915-1918, Cremona Edizioni

- M. Eichta (1997), Braunau 1915-1918, Persico Edizioni

- M. Silvestri (2001), Isonzo 1917, BUR

- J. R. Schindler (2002), Isonzo – Il massacro dimenticato della Grande Guerra, L.E.G.

- Relazione della Commissione d'Inchiesta R. Decreto 12 Gennaio N.35 (1919), Dall'Isonzo al Piave, 24 Ottobre-9 Novembre 1917, Roma, Stabilimento Poligrafico per l'Amministrazione Della Guerra

- G.G. Corbanese, A. Mansutti (2003), Il Friuli, Trieste e l'Istria nel conflitto 1915/1918, Caporetto e l'invasione del Friuli, Del Bianco Editore

- A. Valori (1925), La Guerra Italo-Austriaca, Nicola Zanichelli Editore

- L. Cadorna (1921), La Guerra alla fronte italiana, Treves

- L. Cadorna (1967), Lettere ai famigliari, Arnoldo Mondadori Editore

- R. Bencivenga (1997), La sorpresa strategica di Caporetto, Gaspari Editore

- G.E. Rusconi (2005), L'azzardo del 1915, Il Mulino

- B. Bianchi (2001), La follia e la fuga. Nevrosi di guerra, diserzione e disobbedienza nell'esercito italiano 1915-1918, Bulzoni

  - B. Bianchi (2001), I disobbedienti nella grande guerra, saggio relativo a: «B. Bianchi (2001), La follia e la fuga. Nevrosi di guerra, diserzione e disobbedienza nell'esercito italiano 1915-1918, Bulzoni»

  - Ministero della Difesa, Stato Maggiore dell'Esercito, Ufficio Storico (1967), L'esercito italiano nella Grande Guerra, Volume IV, Le operazioni del 1917

  - Valerio Lintner, A Traveller's History of Italy, The Windrush Press

Photographs:

  - Private collection of Alessandro Gualtieri

  - Private collection of Giovanni Dalle Fusine

  - Private collection of Nicolena Damiani

  - Private collection of Walberto Bortoloso

# Acknowledgments

There are a number of people who have made the publication of this manuscript possible. The authors would like to express their most sincere and profound gratitude to the following persons and organizations:

Lena Damiani
Chester Damiani
Eleuterio Damiani
Tim Damiani
Richard Damiani
Dante Damiani
Scott Patrick Damiani
Elvira Carosi Damiani
Guy J. Damiani (posthumously)
Sally Shapiro-Pellati
Massimiliano Torresan
Paolo Nonino
The Italian Community of Chicago Heights, Illinois, U.S.A.
The Municipality of Acquaviva Picena, Italy
The Municipality of San Benedetto del Tronto, Italy
The Municipality of Doberdò del Lago, Italy

www.ingramcontent.com/pod-product-compliance
Lightning Source LLC
Chambersburg PA
CBHW032300150426
43195CB00008BA/525